making memory books by hand

making memory books by hand

22 PROJECTS TO MAKE, KEEP, AND SHARE

GLOUCESTER MASSACHUSETTS

ROCKPORT PUBLISHERS

KRISTINA FELICIANO

First published in the United States of America by
Quarry Books, an imprint of
Rockport Publishers, Inc.
33 Commercial Street
Gloucester, Massachusetts 01930-5089
Telephone: (978) 282-9590
Fax: (978) 283-2742

Distributed to the book trade and art trade in the
United States by
North Light, an imprint of
F & W Publications
1507 Dana Avenue
Cincinnati, Ohio 45207
Telephone: (800) 289-0963

Other Distribution by
Rockport Publishers, Inc.
Gloucester, Massachusetts 01930-5089

ISBN 1-56496-585-6

10 9 8 7 6 5 4 3 2

Design: The Design Company
Layout: SYP Design & Production
Cover artwork: *Emily and Spot*, by Raymond H. Starr Jr.
              Wedding Photo Album, by Raven Regan
Cover and interior photography by Kevin Thomas

Printed in China.

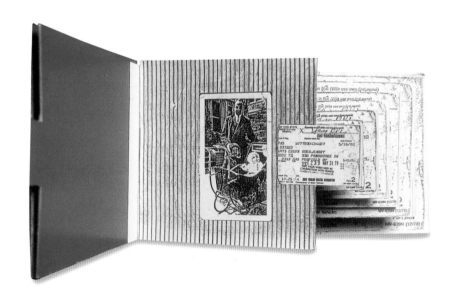

Acknowledgments

The author thanks the many talented artists who contributed
to this book. Without their patience, dedication, and creativity,
this project would not have been possible.

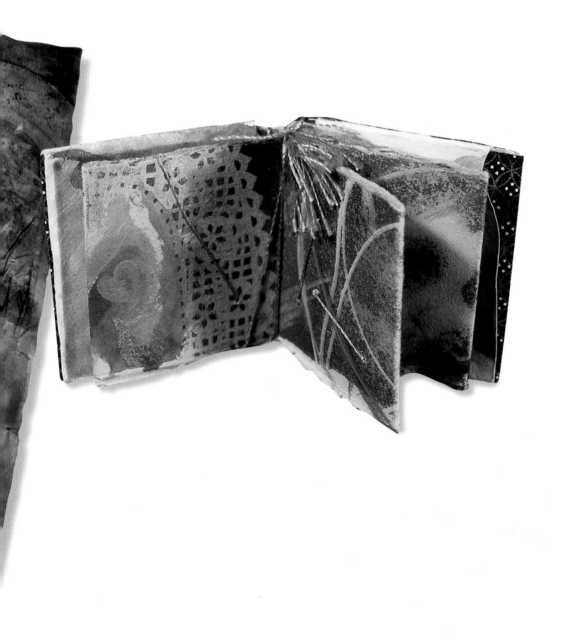

contents

Introduction

Memory books just might be the finest way to celebrate all you hold dear. They're versatile, come in all shapes and sizes (and even test the limits of what a "book" is supposed to look like), and, in the hands of the artists featured in this book, cover a lot of ground. For example, Peter Madden makes handsome, oversized books filled with solvent transfers of memorabilia from his travels abroad. Catherine Badot-Costello incorporated artwork and writings by her family to create a book in honor of her ninety-year-old grandmother. Susan Hensel turned a writing exercise to describe her childhood home into a memory book in the shape of the house.

So many art forms are burdened with rules and with concerns about marketability. These are not the worries of people who make memory books. This is a very personal craft. That means whatever direction a book artist explores is the right one. Snapshots, mementos, and other ephemera—these and a basic understanding of bookmaking are all that is needed.

While it's true that most people are probably already well-equipped to make a memory book, it's also the case that every artist can benefit from inspiration and instruction. That's where *Making Memory Books by Hand* comes in. Divided into four categories—Travel, Personal, Family and Friends, and Special Events—it provides demonstrations by eleven gifted artists that offer something for the

amateur and the professional alike. The steps these artists took to create their books are clearly outlined through color photographs and captions. Plus, all the artists present a variation of their book to illustrate just how versatile their project is. It's easy to follow along with these demonstrations to produce a book just like the one pictured or to simply use these artists' processes as a jumping-off point for an entirely different book.

For a refresher course on bookmaking, stop first at the Basics section. It discusses paper, adhesives, book cloth, tools, and the other items generally used in bookmaking. This section also reviews various ways to make corners, an essential skill for wrapping cover boards with paper or cloth.

For ideas on new approaches to memory books, check out the gallery at the end of each of the four sections. Artists from all over the world contributed their work for this part of the book, and the range of their creativity is impressive. It will be impossible to look at making memory books the same way after taking in these artists' imaginative creations.

Some readers may even be inspired to get started on a book right away—an impulse that absolutely should not be denied.

KRISTINA FELICIANO

Basics

About Paper

When selecting specific papers for a project, ask yourself the following questions: Is the paper appropriate for the book's purpose? Does the paper help express the look or feel you want your book to have? Does the paper complement the other materials used in the book? Finally, ask the people working at paper stores and art stores for advice. They are usually quite knowledgeable and will be glad to help.

While modern technology has made it possible to produce mass quantities of paper cheaply, there are still papers being made around the world by hand using natural fibers and old-world techniques. These decorative papers work well as covers, end sheets, or even interior pages. A visit to a local paper store or a well-stocked art store will reveal the tremendous assortment of papers you can choose from. They can be thin enough to see through, such as many Japanese rice papers, or as thick as the cardboard of a corrugated box. They can be as smooth as silk tissue paper or as rough as tree bark.

All paper has one common characteristic—the grain. The grain indicates the arrangement or direction of the fibers. A book will be stronger, less likely to warp, and easier to fold if the grain of all your papers is parallel with the spine. Companies often label which way the grain runs. For machine-made commercial paper, the

grain usually runs the length of the paper. If the grain is not listed, you can test it by bending or folding the paper. A piece of paper folds easily and without cracking if the crease is parallel with the grain. If you fold a piece of paper and it shows signs of cracking along the crease, you know the grain runs in the opposite direction. If you still cannot determine which way the grain runs, cut a small piece and wet it. As the paper dries, it will begin to bend in the direction of the grain. For handmade papers, the grain is of less concern. It is arranged in many different directions, and is therefore not as clearly defined as in machine-made commercial paper.

Materials and Supplies

In addition to various kinds of paper, there are a few other materials and supplies needed to complete the projects in this book.

Cloth

Most books use cloth for all or part of the cover. Binder's cloth is a strong, durable cloth with a paper backing. It can be purchased at binderies and paper stores. Other types of cloth can also be used. If the cloth you want has a loose weave or is very thin, it must be backed with paper to give it added strength and provide a surface on which to spread glue. Rice paper makes good backing material.

Adhesives

Cloth and paper are adhered to a book using glue or paste. For the projects described in this book, polyvinyl acetate (PVA) is recommended. It is white, dries clear, and can be thinned with water. You can substitute PVA with other white paper glues. You can also use wheat paste, rice paste, or paste made from cornstarch. To mix your own paste, look for recipe books that show you how.

Thread

The binding on some of the projects in this book is sewn. Professional binders use linen thread, which is strong but rather expensive. As a substitute, use thick cotton thread, embroidery silk, or even dental floss if the book is small. A variety of ribbons, cords, or twine can add color to your spine. Avoid using sewing thread, which breaks easily.

Cover Board or Binder's Board

The front and back covers of most books are made with heavy paper or cardboard. Davy board, a type of cover board used by binders, can be purchased from local binderies or through catalogs. Cover boards vary in thickness from 0.02 inch (a thin board) to 0.147 inch (a thick board). The latter is almost impossible to cut by hand. For practical purposes, the thickness of the cover boards should be about 0.08 or 0.09 inch, except in cases when a thin board, such as shirt board (0.02), is required.

Scrap Paper

Making books by hand can get a bit messy. Use large scraps of paper as a barrier to protect your materials and work surface while gluing and cutting. Remember to discard wet barriers and replace them with clean, dry ones. Rolls of wax paper and craft paper wrappers are an inexpensive source of protective paper.

Sandpaper

Medium sandpaper can be used to round any sharp corners or irregular edges of your cover boards.

Damp Cloth

Keep a damp cloth handy while gluing. Use it to clean sticky fingers so that you do not get any unwanted glue on finished surfaces.

Tools

This list includes many of the tools needed to complete the projects in this book. Not every tool listed here is required for every project, of course. Some of the projects may require additional tools—such as a letterpress, electric drill, or a computer.

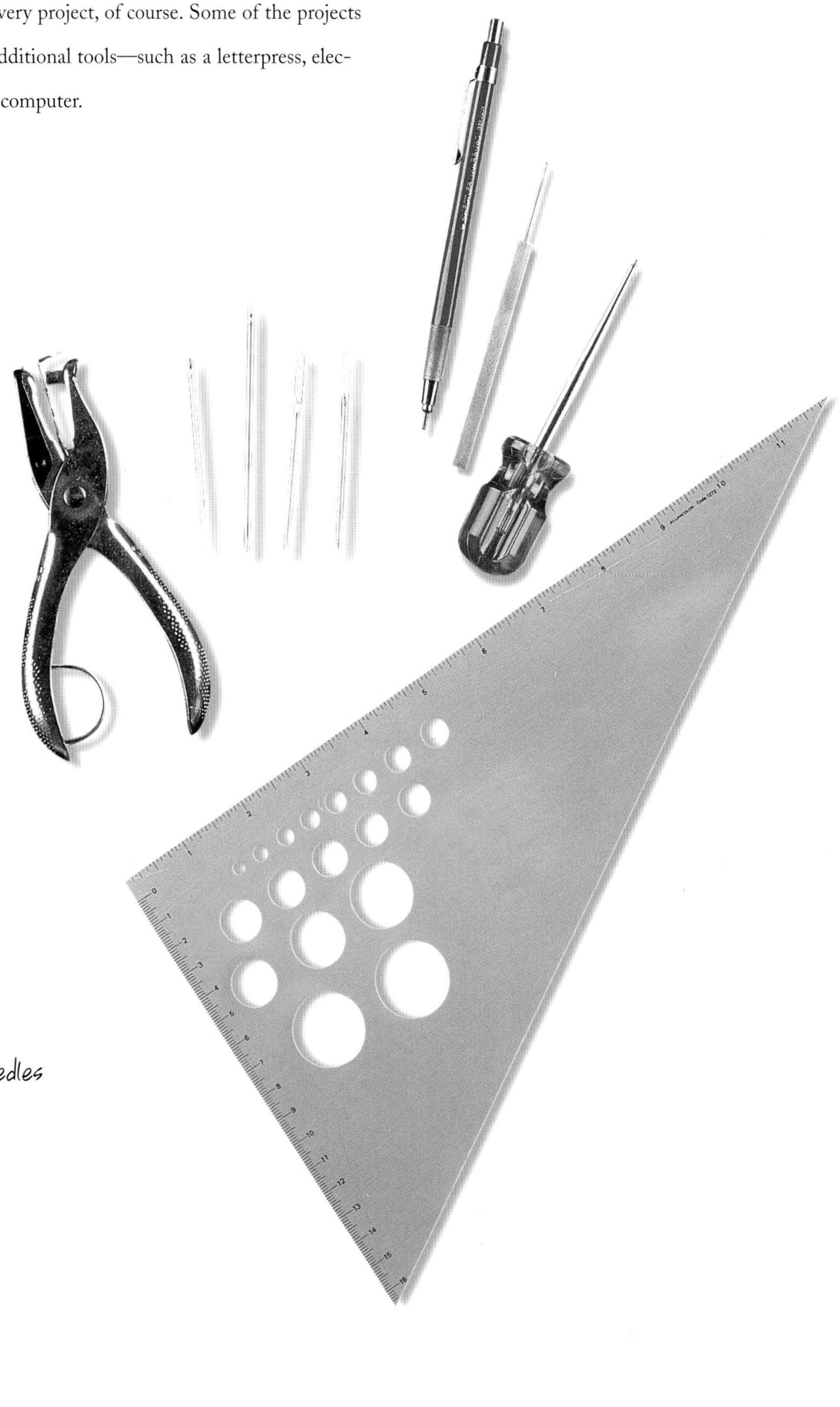

Square angle rule

Assorted craft needles

Pencil

Hole punch

Needle tool

Awl

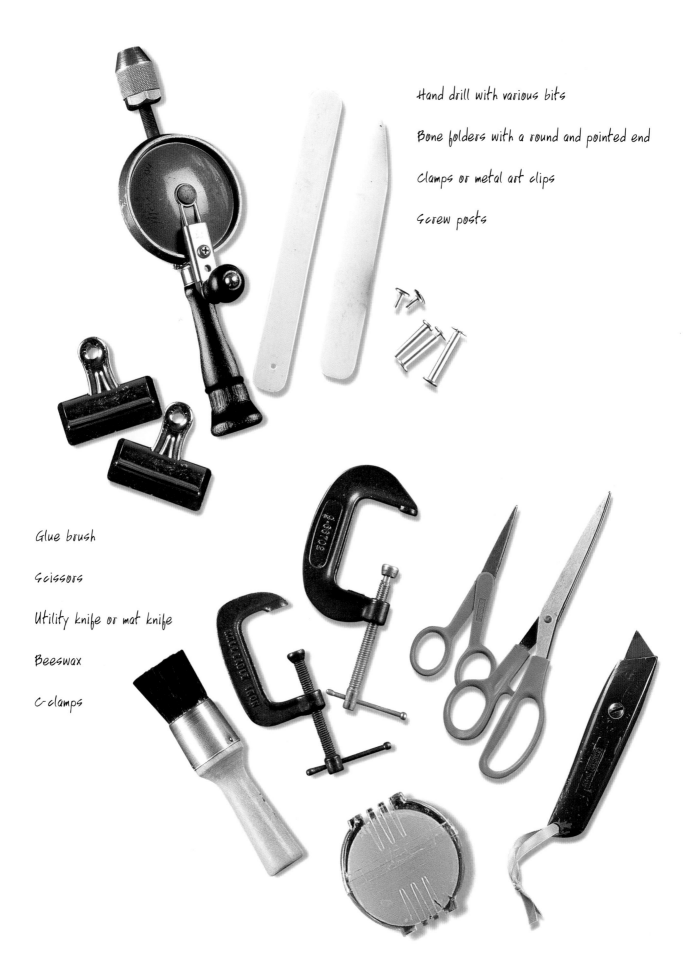

Hand drill with various bits

Bone folders with a round and pointed end

Clamps or metal art clips

Screw posts

Glue brush

Scissors

Utility knife or mat knife

Beeswax

C-clamps

How to Make Corners

For many of the projects in this book, cover boards are wrapped with either cloth or paper. As it requires practice to make neat corners, take time to study the three methods of wrapping corners described below. For each method, make sure you cut the material no closer than $1/4$" (.5 cm) to the corners of the board.

Method One: For Thin Paper or Cloth

Cut off the corners of your material at a diagonal fold, and glue one side of the material down on the board.

Use a bone folder to press the paper down at a slight angle over the corner.

Glue and fold the paper on the adjacent side in the same way.

Method Two: For Thick or Brittle Paper

Cut off the corners of your paper at a diagonal fold, and glue one side down on the board. Then, with scissors, cut a straight line from the fold of the cloth that extends to the corner of the board.

With a bone folder or a finger, tuck the small triangular piece you have just created around the corner onto the lip of the adjacent side. Snip off the peak that has formed with scissors as shown.

Glue and fold the adjacent side down on the board.

Method Three: For Cloth or Paper

Cut a square into the cloth or paper as shown. Cut carefully so that one corner of the square remains attached to the material.

Glue and fold the square over the inside of the board.

Glue and fold the adjacent sides of the material down on the inside of the board.

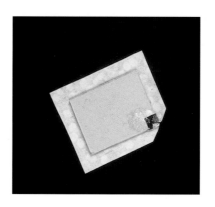

travel memory books

It's amazing the things that can be collected from a vacation: postcards, brochures, ticket stubs. It's the kind of stuff that usually winds up in a shoe box shoved somewhere in the far corners of the closet. Why not sort through that box and use the best of the lot in a memory book?

Or maybe you're a traveler of the armchair variety. There's a destination dear to your heart, so you make a travel book all about the place.

And let's not forget the travel diary, a type of memory book notable for its spontaneity. In it you can note your impressions, make sketches, and paste local headlines.

ed by an additional burden:
ern belle mystique.
isolated by the size of
between homes.
rned well how to survive.
, may scare cowboys.

French Travelogue

BASED ON A PROJECT BY PETER MADDEN

"A book is a journey, and I almost always make my journeys into books," says artist Peter Madden, whose passion for travelogues was handed down from his mother (she kept meticulous scrapbook journals of every trip the family took for over twenty years). When he travels, Madden tries to keep an open mind about what he might collect for his book, absorbing, assimilating, collecting, roaming, and recording what he sees in photographs, sketches, and notes. What he winds up with might just look like a pile of junk—maps, postcards, rubbings, ticket stubs, newspaper clippings, and so on—but he edits it down to create richly evocative books whose every detail captures the essence of the place and his time there.

What You Need

Thin-gauge pine or plywood

Copper

Nails

Hammer

Saw

Drill

Nuts and bolts

Cardboard template

Brass hinges

Wood stain

Photocopies of mementos and solvent

Stamp made from an old cork

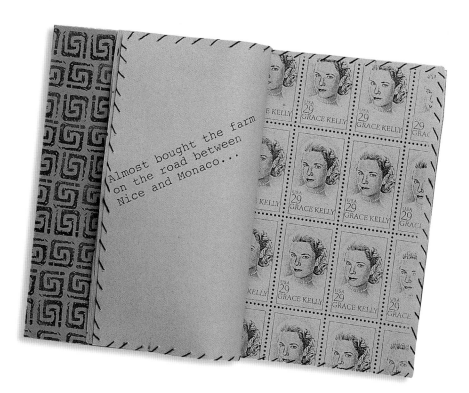

Almost bought the farm on the road between Nice and Monaco...

step-by-step

1. Making the covers

Begin by making a cardboard template the size of the book, to get a sense of what the book will eventually look like and to scale the pages. Cut the front and back covers, and the spine strip (which you can estimate by eye). The cover of Madden's book, for example, is 7 3/4" x 10 1/2" (19.5 cm x 27 cm), so he cut a spine strip that is 3/4" (2 cm) wide, which worked aesthetically and gave him enough room to fill the pages as planned.

2. Decorating the covers

Next, decorate the cover of the book and glue endpapers to the inside of both covers. To decorate his book, Madden transferred a rubbing of an old embossed leather book cover that he found at a flea market in Paris onto the wooden cover and stained it lightly to give it an antique look. On the inside of the wooden cover he glued handmade endpapers that he decorated with a handmade stamp—a bottle cork that he cut into a simple shape.

3. Aging and installing the hinges

Once the front and back covers have been decorated inside and out, hinge them to the spine strip using little brass hinges from the hardware store. Madden aged the hinges by oxidizing them with ammonia to darken and stain them. He then added copper stripping to the edges of the covers for a more finished look.

4. Filling the pages

Using solvent transfers is Madden's favorite method of adding content to his books. In this case, he made transfers from rubbings (also known as frottage) taken from textured buildings or signs where he vacationed. When the content of the book is finished, use rubber bands to hold the pages and covers in place while drilling the two holes necessary to bolt the book together.

5. Binding

Countersink the nuts and bolts in the two holes that have been drilled through the entire package: front cover, entire block of pages, and back cover. Madden then covered the holes with small diamond shapes cut from oxidized copper and nailed to the spine strip.

Variation
GREECE BOOK

10" x 8 ½" (25 cm x 22 cm)

For a slightly more organic look, Madden actually sewed through the binding, rather than using nuts and bolts. The found objects dangling from the spine— cherry pits, keys, religious medals, and sea shells—enhance the book's immediacy.

Guatemala Trip Journal

BASED ON A PROJECT BY LAURA BLACKLOW

Artist Laura Blacklow uses very little manipulation in her travel books. Rather than make color copies of her snapshots, for example, she uses the actual snapshots. The result is a book that feels entirely personal; a shoe box of memories made into book form. This is not to say that she doesn't pay attention to the book's aesthetics. She fusses over paper selection and is mindful of the juxtaposition of images: A page of Polaroids may face a full-page sketch, or pictures may be arranged into a panorama, as in this book, *Guatemala Trip Journal.* But her travel books themselves are slightly rough-hewn, as if they've been around.

What You Need

Medium-weight acid-free paper for pages

Heavyweight acid-free paper for cover

Ruler

Single-edge razor blade or stencil knife

Four thick, large rubber bands

Scissors

Bone folder

90-degree right triangle

PVA glue

step-by-step

1. Making the pages

Working with acid-free paper (acid can react with the chemicals in a photograph and result in yellowing and staining), mark off pages measuring 5 1/2" x 9 3/4" (14 cm x 24.5 cm), adding a 1/2" (1 cm) to the binding edge only. Score the pages lightly with a utility knife and fold each page at the 1/2" (1 cm) mark at the binding edge. This tab allows you to include Polaroids and other items of reasonable thickness in the book without preventing it from closing flat.

2. Making a pocket page

To measure for the height of the pocket page, double the height of the other pages, then subtract 1/4" (.5 cm) so that it is the same height as the other pages but slightly lower in front where the mementos will be inserted. The pocket page is the same width as the other pages—with 1/2" (1 cm) included for the spine and another 1/2" (1 cm) added to the right side of the page for the seam of the pocket. Cut a small triangle at the bottom right corner and a small rectangle at the top right corner to create tabs to form the pocket. These tabs can be eliminated to create a page that folds down into the book.

3. Making a fold-out page

Blacklow also made a fold-out page in black for a panorama consisting of Polaroids she took of the landscape. To make a fold-out page, cut a piece of paper twice as long as a single page minus 1" (3 cm)—not forgetting to add the 1/2" (1 cm)—necessary for the binding side—so that it can fold in without interfering with the binding.

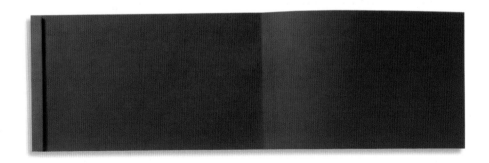

4. Cutting the cover

Cut the cover, which should be of heavier paper than the inside pages, 1/8" (.3 cm) larger than the inside pages to protect them. Score the folds for binding.

5. Binding

Stack the pages, taking care to line up all the tabs, and use heavy rubber bands to hold the stack together. Put the stacked pages into the cover and measure out five evenly spaced holes (these can be made with an electric or hand drill). Sew the binding (Blacklow used gold embroidery thread), starting at the center and working your way back.

Variation

SOUTHWEST TERRITORIES

7 ¼" x 8" (18.5 cm x 20 cm)

The signatures of Blacklow's book about her travels in the Southwest are similar in construction to those of the *Guatemala Trip Journal,* but the binding is more complex, so that at first it looks like a store-bought book. It, too, is filled with her snapshots of the people she met and the places she visited, as well as fragments of text that unfold in a stream-of-consciousness style. The quilted cover features the shapes of Texas, New Mexico, and Arizona, the three states she visited.

Travel Memories

A GALLERY OF BOOKS

1.

2.

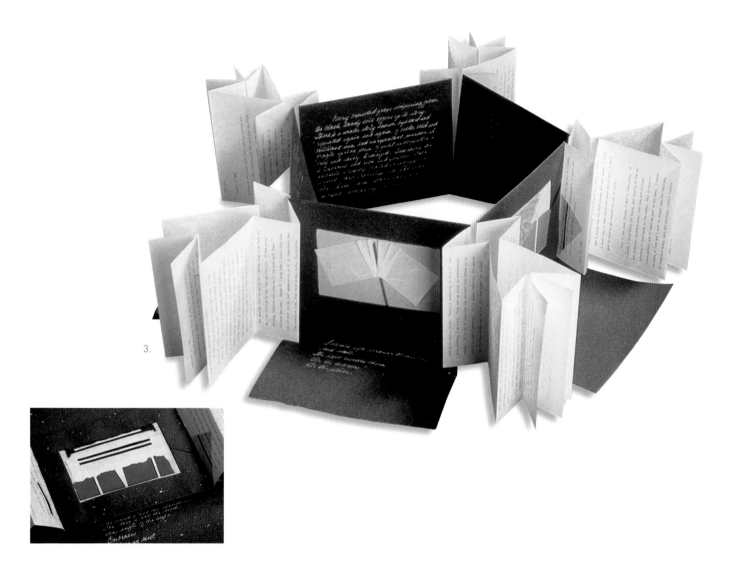

3.

1. FRIENDSHIP, VITALITY, AND STRENGTH

Lonnie Graham

Photogravure images with handset type.
Box: 12" x 11 1/2" x 13 1/2"
(30 cm x 29 cm x 34 cm);
books: 9 5/8" x 7 1/4" (24 cm x 18.5 cm)

Friendship, Vitality, and Strength is the culmination of Graham's pilgrimages to Kenya and other parts of East Africa over a fifteen-year period. It consists of three books—each concertina-bound and covered with handmade tapa cloth imported from East Africa—contained in a box handcrafted from East African wenge and zebra wood.

2. 36 VIEWS OF THE EMPIRE STATE BUILDING

Béatrice Coron

Accordion-fold paper-cutting book.
11" x 9" x 4" (28 cm x 23 cm x 10 cm)

Coron, who has adapted paper-cutting to many different formats, often collaborates with writers. Here, she juxtaposed poems by Marcia Newfield with scenes of the Empire State Building in New York City. The poetry adds to the wistfulness of many of the images. For a picture of a man fishing alone under a bridge, with the iconic building in the distance, the text reads: "Sometimes the fish here are so small, I throw them all back. Sometimes they're just right."

3. MINNESOTA LANDBOOK

Barbara Harman

Tuxedo parchment, Larroque constellation paper and collages made of assorted Japanese papers. 7" (18 cm) pentagram, closed

Harman's book, which folds completely flat and fits into an envelope, contains three texts: a journal about her experiences when she moved to Minnesota; a narrative text about the state's landscape; and a poem about a personal relationship that parallels the other two texts. This is the last in a series of books the artist made about regional landscapes and relationships.

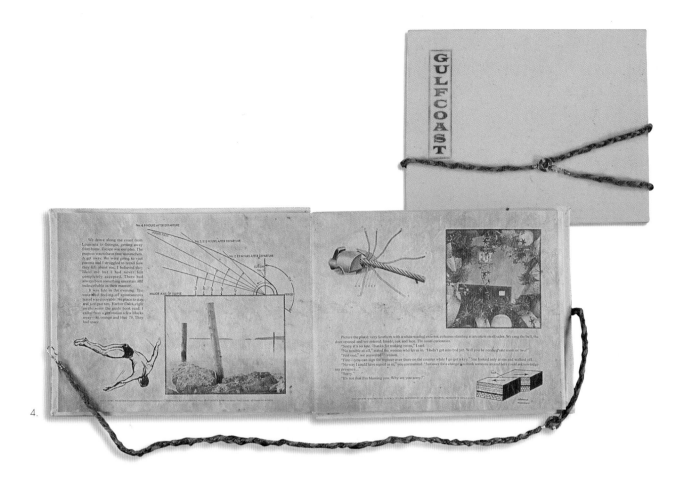

4.

1. BOCA NEGRA CANYON: TRAIL GUIDE

Jody Alexander

Handbound, with non-adhesive binding, and featuring block prints on handmade paper. 7" x 5" (18 cm x 13 cm)

Alexander made four one-of-a-kind books as a result of a trip she made to New Mexico. In *Boca Negra Canyon: Trail Guide,* she wanted to give the viewer the feeling of what it was like to be among the deep-brown volcanic rocks of the canyon, on whose walls are etched ancient petroglyphs. She also wanted to convey how remarkable it is that people are permitted to walk freely and unsupervised among these treasures.

2. THE COVERED BRIDGES OF BUCKS COUNTY, PA

3. THE WINDING ROADS OF IRELAND

Jane Conneen

Hand-colored drawings on Hahnemuhle Bugre paper. 2" x 2 ¼" (5 cm x 5.5 cm)

Conneen does all her own illustrations, taking photographs during her travels and later making pen-and-ink drawings for use in her books.

4. GULFCOAST

David Schlater

Accordion-fold book of 23 pages; original text and photographs/found images; printed on Japanese paper using Van Dyke Brown photographic process. 8" x 10" (20 cm x 25 cm)

Gulfcoast is based on two very different journeys the artist made from New Orleans to Alabama. One trip he made with a person he was dating, and the other was with his mother after attending his father's funeral. He merged both experiences to relate a story of discovery, loss, death, and recovery.

1.

2.

3.

1. JOURNEY TALES

Ann Kresge

Seven color-viscosity etchings and letter-press on rag paper, housed in a handmade folio box. 15" x 11" (38 cm x 28 cm)

A travel book in a metaphorical sense, *Journey Tales* consists of etchings Kresge made based on stories and masks by storyteller and sculptor Suzanne Benton. The book visually relates women's stories from the verbal traditions of different cultures around the world.

2. WISH YOU WERE HERE

Emily Martin

Mailing envelopes purchased in England, bound with pencils in a piano-hinge format. 6" x 8" x 6" (15 cm x 20 cm x 15 cm)

The envelopes contain all the postcards—three each day—Martin mailed home while visiting England. The postcards tell the story of her travels, and she included ticket stubs and other related mementos to further describe her experiences. The book is composed entirely of articles collected from her trip—even the pencils used in the binding.

3. THE SHORE

Jill Timm

Accordion-fold book, with color photos, shells, and oat grass. 2 3/8" x 3" (5.5 cm x 8 cm)

Timm's *The Shore* was inspired by a trip she took to the Texas seaside and, appropriately, includes not only her photos (which she scanned and then manipulated in Photoshop) but also oat grass and shells she collected.

3.

1. MAUI JOURNAL

Carolynn Dallaire

Mixed media. 6 $^3/_8$" x 5 $^3/_4$"
(17 cm x 14.5 cm)

Dallaire's travel journal shows how diverse materials can be put to creative use. *Maui Journal* features not only the artist's watercolor illustrations and her husband's vacation photos but also related postcards, business cards from their favorite restaurants and galleries, and clippings from tourist magazines.

2. BACKCOUNTRY TRAVEL PACK

Phil Sultz

Mixed media, including rice and mulberry paper, birch bark, red rosin. Pack: 12" x 4" (30 cm x 10 cm); box: 12 $^1/_4$" x 4 $^1/_2$" (31 cm x 11 cm)

Sultz, who has traveled extensively on foot and on horseback through the Rocky Mountains, made this stacked-page journal for recording notes, collecting samples of vegetation, and making sketches. It's meant to be carried in a backpack or saddlebag.

3. BOOK OF FIRE AND LIGHT

Pamela Moore

Copper pages and wood. 8" x 8" x 8" x 1" (20 cm x 20 cm x 20 cm x 3 cm)

Moore, who years ago left the U.S. to live in Spain, made this book as an homage to the desert of Arizona, where she lived for several years as a college student. The desert and copper light there influenced her later work in copper, she says. The *Book of Fire and Light* is a celebration of the landscape that inspired her but that she is no longer able to visit on a regular basis. Each of the pages is sanded in a different manner, and the light reflects on them in a way, the artist says, that echoes a night campfire, the intense red of Arizona's skies, and the endless miles of desert landscape.

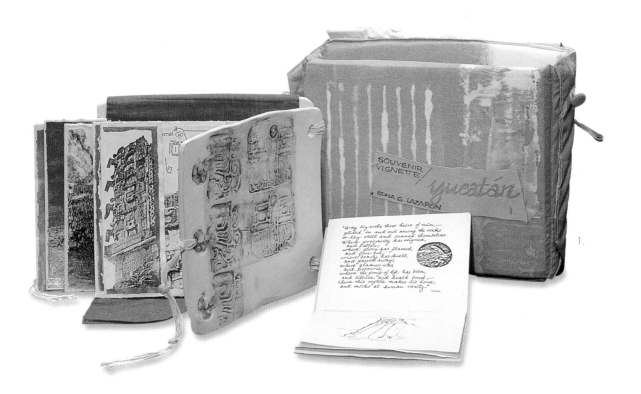

1.

2.

3.

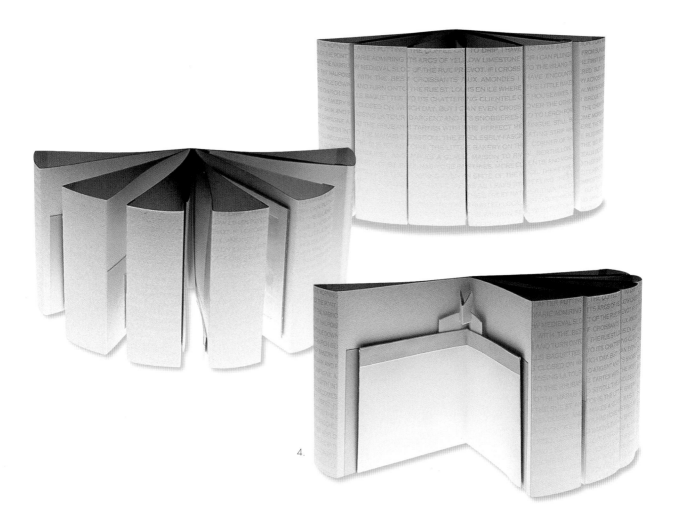

4.

1. SOUVENIR VIGNETTE/YUCATAN

Edna Lazaron

Padded case containing six-page booklet with ceramic covers and consisting of Twin-rocker paper, color copies, and the artist's original photos. 8" x 10" (20 cm x 25 cm)

2. SOUVENIR VIGNETTE/ CLASSIC MAYA

Edna Lazaron

Padded case containing four-page booklet featuring artist's own photographs. 6 1/2" x 7 1/2" (17 cm x 19 cm)

Lazaron, an avid traveler, has an ongoing book series she calls "Travel-og Series: Souvenir Vignettes." Her travel books have a scrapbook aesthetic, incorporating sketches she has made on location, fellow travelers' photos as well as her own, and hand-lettered quotations from books related to her trip.

3. ITALIAN PLACES

Evelyn Eller

Mixed media, including wooden box with collaged shelves. 7 1/2" x 5" x 6 1/2" (19 cm x 13 cm x 17 cm)

Inspired by the artist's time as a student in Italy. this book consists of an antique wooden box originally made to store photographs. Eller made shelves for the box and collaged each one with images of a single Italian city and related maps. Each shelf can be pulled out and admired.

4. IN THE MORNING

Mei-Ling Hom

Five wedge-shaped pages with silkscreened pop-up illustrations. 10 3/4" x 6" (27.5 cm x 15 cm)

The text that serves as a decorative pattern on the outside of the book— "Baguettes...croissants"—says it all in this travel book about strolling through the back streets of Paris in search of small neighborhood bakeries.

personal memory books

Technically, all memory books are "personal"—they all relate
to the artist's life in one way or another. But for our
purposes, personal memory books are about examining
the self—the artist getting to know the artist.

Consider the diary. Most people think of diaries as something very predictable: You diligently record the events of
your life in it. But life is hardly predictable, so it follows that
your journal shouldn't be, either. Don't be afraid to muck it
up a little—draw in it, paint in it, make collages in it. Some
people even make personal memory books about specific
experiences in their life, like moving to a new house.

Personal memory books give artists the ultimate opportunity
to indulge themselves, and there's a lot to be learned in the
process. Who knows what kind of discoveries you can make
along the way?

My House

BASED ON A PROJECT BY SUSAN HENSEL

My *House* started as a written exercise that artist Susan Hensel gave herself to describe her childhood home as if discussing it with a stranger. She then realized there were ways to tie in related writings about her mother. "When you take the time to reflect on certain aspects of your life," she says, "other memories and emotions often well up unexpectedly." So her writing about her home then turned into a book in the shape of a house that looks back on her mother and the rest of her family—even her dog—when she was five years old. Hensel says she remembers the knotty-pine walls of her house in upstate New York, the way the light filtered in through the door, and how the slate floor outside looked when it had been washed down. These are some of the images she evokes in *My House*, which features printed images of a house she encountered as an adult that reminded her of her childhood home.

What You Need

10 sheets black Canson Mi-Teintes paper, 8 ½" x 14" (22 cm x 36 cm)

10 sheets Wausau Royal Fiber, 8 ½" x 14" (22 cm x 36 cm)

Two pieces black mat board, 8 ½" x 7" (22 cm x 18 cm)

One roll heat-activated adhesive

PVA glue

Dry iron

Utility knife

Ruler

Cutting surface

Bone folder

Small, flat brush

Waste paper (such as an old phone book)

step-by-step

1. Making the pages

Cut 10 sheets of Wausau Royal Fiber at 8 ½" x 14" (22 cm x 36 cm) each to use as the pages. Print, draw on, paint, or otherwise decorate them, keeping the design in the shape of a house. (Hensel printed an image of a house with an image of herself as a child.)

2. Reinforcing the pages (part 1)

Next, cut 10 sheets of black Canson Mi-Teintes paper measuring 8 ½" x 14" (22 cm x 36 cm). Use this paper as reinforcement for the printed pages and as a decorative element, as the black provides a handsome contrast with the brown pages you've decorated. Then apply heat-activated adhesive to the back of the pages, following the manufacturer's directions.

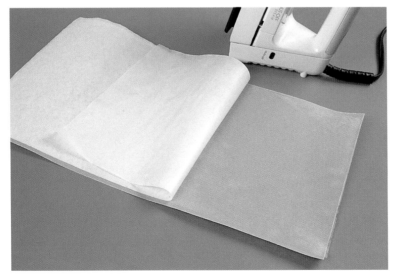

3. Reinforcing the pages (part 2)

Remove the backing from the adhesive. Using the backing as a pressing cloth, iron the black paper and the pages together.

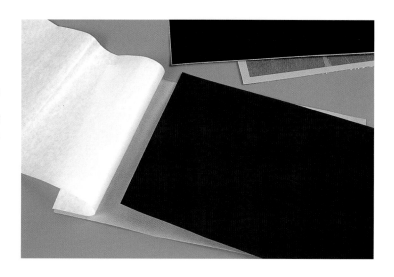

4. Reinforcing the pages (part 3)

Now trim the excess paper away from the images so that each page is uniformly in the shape of a house, and put aside two pages to use as endpapers.

5. Collating the pages

Use a bone folder or blunt butter knife to score the center line of each of the pages. Then fold the pages in half along the scored line and stack the folded sheets in the order they will appear in the book.

6. Gluing the pages together

First, apply a strip of glue to the back of the right-hand fore edge (the open edge) of the first page. Use waste paper (such as the pages of an old phone book) to prevent excess glue from ruining the other pages. Then carefully place the next page onto this strip of glue and rub it down to make sure it will stick. Repeat this process for all of the pages to create an accordion-fold book.

7. Making the covers

Cut two 8 ½" x 7" (22 cm x 18 cm) pieces of black mat board to use as the covers. Apply heat-activated adhesive to the endpapers and adhere them to the mat board, once again using the removed backing cloth from the adhesive as a pressing cloth. Trim the covers to the required size.

8. Adhering the covers to the book

Next, apply heat-activated adhesive to the back of the cover boards and iron the first page of the book to the front cover. Repeat this process for the back cover to finish the book.

9. Making a box for the book

Make a box for the book, as a way to store it and easily transport it. Hensel made her box out of Davy board that she decorated with acrylic paint, modeling paste, and crackle medium.

Variation
I LOOKED DOWN THE HALL

8 ½" x 5 ½" (22 cm x 14 cm)

Halls have great metaphorical significance for Hensel. One day in her current home, she walked out of her office and looked down the hall and was overwhelmed by all her remembered experiences. This was the inspiration for *I Looked Down the Hall,* in which, the artist says, "the rug in the hall symbolizes a river of tears, a river of healing, and a river of baptism."

Journal 1

BASED ON A PROJECT BY JOAN DUFF-BOHRER

Artist Joan Duff-Bohrer takes a free-form approach to journal-making. While her book-binding process is fairly defined (she always makes paste paper to decorate the covers and uses the coptic binding method to assemble her books), her method for filling the pages is best described as anything goes. Above all, this artist believes that a journal should be whatever the owner wants to make it, and all worries about keeping the pages pristine should be cast aside.

What You Need

Paste paper

Scissors

Bone folder

Utility knife

Cornstarch

Wax paper

Electric drill

Waxed linen thread

Curved needle

Pliers

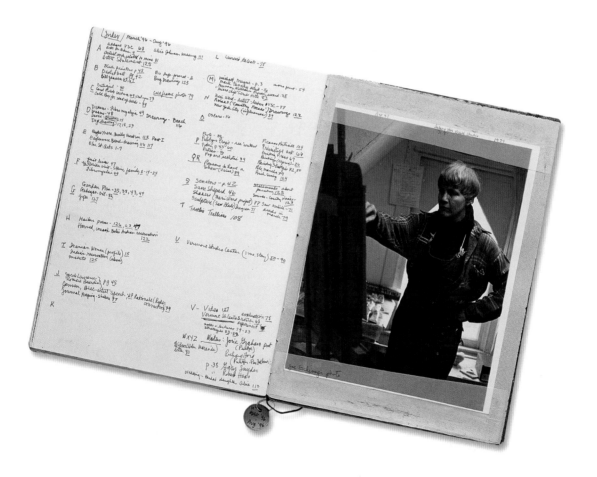

step-by-step

1. Making paste paper for covers

Make paste paper, let it dry, and iron it flat. Paste paper is made from a mixture of flour, water, and pigment. It's a great way to design patterns and colors and is ideal for Duff-Bohrer's journals, which are extremely individual.

2. Decorating the covers

Choose a section of the paste paper, using a frame finder cut from cardboard, for the covers. (Duff-Bohrer uses cornstarch glue, which she makes herself, as an adhesive.) Even her endpaper is handmade: Here Duff-Bohrer cut endpaper from some of her old sketches and pasted it onto the book board. Next weight down the covers, with wax paper in between them, and let them sit overnight so they dry flat.

3. Preparing the signatures and spine covers

First fold the signatures (the paper should be ¹/₂" [1 cm] smaller in length and height when folded than the cover size). There are eight signatures of four folded sheets each. Note that the spines for the first and last signature should be cut differently, with a full page on the outside of each to be used for a title sheet at the beginning or for a decorative page at the end.

4. Binding

Using a handmade template, poke holes through the signatures and spines. (Duff-Bohrer recommends making the holes no more than 3" [8 cm] apart.) Drill holes in the covers and then align the entire package and wrap it so it will stay in place when sewing. Duff-Bohrer used the traditional coptic binding method.

5. Filling the pages

Duff-Bohrer's journals also function as personal photo albums. Here, the artist is pictured at her easel.

Variation

JOURNAL 2

12" x 9" (30 cm x 23 cm)

Journals are not just for text. Duff-Bohrer likes to include notes to herself, clippings from magazines, photos, sketches—all manner of scraps and mementos that relate to her life.

Modus Vivendi

BASED ON A PROJECT BY MARIA PISANO

Artist Maria Pisano was born in Italy, and it remains very dear to her. She says going back is like making a discovery, and she tries to visit a different city each trip. Like many artists who travel to Italy, Pisano comes away from these visits inspired to create art. But because the country holds so much personal significance for her, she is also inspired to reflect on her heritage. In *Modus Vivendi* (Latin for way of living), Pisano explores her past and present and that of her family by way of surrealistic photocollages that combine old family photos and current vacation snapshots. It's an example of how a book's structure can be as significant as what the book contains. *Modus Vivendi* unfolds continuously until you get to its center—representing how memories unfold and unravel, almost as if with their own momentum.

What You Need

Rives BFK paper

Polymer plates

Photographs

Computer with Photoshop

Letterpress

Linen thread

Paste paper

Etching press

Utility knife

Ruler

step-by-step

1. Creating images for each page

Pisano's book consists of letterpress prints. To try this, select photos you've taken (Pisano used ones she shot in Italy) along with old family photos, scan them into a computer using a flatbed scanner, and make a photocollage from them using Photoshop. Have a service bureau (a photo-processing store should be able to do it or at least direct you to a service bureau) output the files as negatives to use to make prints.

2. Making plates

Place the negative on a polymer plate (a light-sensitive plate used for printmaking that can be purchased at most art-supply stores) and expose the plate to ultraviolet light. This sets the positive image on the plate. Then rinse the plate to remove the excess polymer, and let it dry. Expose the plate to ultraviolet light a second time to set and harden the polymer, making the plate ready for printing.

3. Making pages and printing images

To create a book that will fold out continuously, adjust the width of the pages according to their placement in the book. For example, make page one 11" high and 8 1/2" wide (28 cm x 22 cm) and each subsequent page 1/8" (.3 cm) smaller than the previous one. The last page should measure 7 1/2" (19 cm) wide (the height remains constant throughout). Use a letterpress to print your images in black ink.

4. Binding the book

To decorate the cover, Pisano used a collograph plate (a printing plate whose surface has been built and is then incised with the image) and an etching press with silver and black ink. Try using a paste-paper pattern, as Pisano did, to decorate the inside of the cover. To bind the book, cut four paste-paper binding strips of Rives BFK paper to 11" x ³/₄" (28 cm x 2 cm) and fold them down the center. Pair the pages, with the image side facing in, and use 3M series 2-0300 archival double-sided tape to join the paste-paper strips to each pair of pages until all the pages are attached to each other.

5. Finishing the book

Sew the text block to the cover (Pisano used a five-hole pamphlet stitch).

Variation
ECHOES

Case: 8 ¹/₂" x 6" x ³/₄" (22 cm x 15 cm x 2 cm); book: 8" x 6" x ³/₄" (21 cm x 15 cm x 2 cm)

Like *Modus Vivendi, Echoes* requires the reader to unravel it, removing the book from its case, and then from a clear plastic cover, to reveal the collection of text (including a letter written by the artist's young son while visiting Pompeii) and family photos.

Personal Memories

1.

1. IT STARTS WITH A TABLEAU

Sandy Groebner

Accordion-fold binding, with hardcovers coated in beeswax, and photographs; housed in a wooden box. 7" x 11" (18 cm x 28 cm) closed

Groebner culled the text for this book from various sources and arranged them in a stream-of-consciousness style for a dreamlike autobiographical narrative.

2. BOOK OF TRANSFORMATION

Donna Marie deCreeft

Mixed media, including Tibetan rice paper, India ink, acrylic paint, collage, linoleum prints, monoprints, and stamp printing. 10 1/2" x 11 1/2" (27 cm x 29 cm)

DeCreeft calls her books diaries of her unconscious. *The Book of Transformation,* for example, refers symbolically to a year of intense change in her life, using what the artist calls images of potential—seeds, pods, chrysalis, and wings—to suggest her transformation.

3. DREAM LOG

Béatrice Coron

Confetti text paper with photocopied images, 18 pages. 5 1/2" x 8 1/2" (14 cm x 22 cm)

Coron's dream journal features illustrations she made from paper-cuttings and then photocopied. The pages alternate colors, from yellow, to rust, to tan, with a red cover. Charms hang from extra thread left after sewing the binding.

1.

3.

1. UNTITLED (YOUTH PROJECT BOOK)

Laura Blacklow

Cover with a cotton quilt square, plastic binding, pages of rag paper, original black-and-white photos. 8" x 8" (20 cm x 20 cm)

While a graduate student, Blacklow spent a year working with inner-city teenagers in an art-therapy program sponsored by the National Institutes of Mental Health. This is her journal from that time. It includes photos she took of some of the kids she worked with and befriended. She was not required to do the journal for the program; she says she made it for herself to try to capture what the kids meant to her and what she was learning from them.

2. LETTERS NEVER SENT 1 (JULIA)

Bonnie Stahlecker

Six-panel accordion-fold book; abaca paper with over-beaten pigmented pulp design; letterpress, monoprint, collage, and Prisma-colors. 4 $^7/_8$" x 2 $^3/_4$" (13 cm x 7 cm) closed; 4 $^7/_8$" x 14" x 1 $^1/_2$" (13 cm x 36 cm x 4 cm) when displayed

Stahlecker has made a number of books on the theme of what she calls mind letters—letters she composes in her mind but that will exist tangibly only in the form of a book. Fittingly, these books are somewhat mysterious (she writes text through wet paint and a letterpress label, as if to diffuse it further) and often contain little surprises (this one has reversed pop-ups in the peak folds).

3. THE BOOK OF LETTERS (DAS BUCH DER BRIEFE)

Laurie Snyder

Color photocopies of collages, 96 pages, hardbound in linen and paste paper. 11" x 8 $^1/_2$" (28 cm x 22 cm)

Snyder made color photocopies of collages she constructed from letters, telegrams, photographs, fabrics, post-cards, stamps and the like. She then inlaid into each collage a vellum page of text, in the style of a letter, that expresses mixed feelings about her German-American, Jewish, and Christian heritage. Most of the corre-spondence in this book was between her parents, who fled Germany on the brink of World War II.

1.

2.

3.

1. AUGUST BOOK AND BOX

Susan Share

Paper, cloth, photographs, acrylic, water-color, crayon, and collage. 9" x 6" x 1 ½" (23 cm x 15 cm x 4 cm)

Share created this diary in exactly one month: from August 1 to August 30, 1980. Traveling with a drawing kit consisting of crayons, pencils, paints, colored pencils, glue, and an eraser, she did much of the artwork while on trains and buses en route to visit her uncle, Harvey, who was vacationing in Ogunquit, Maine. Share also collected train and museum admission tickets, labels from food packages and drinks she bought, old family photos, ID cards, and other related materials for her diary.

2. DIARIES WITH WRAPPER

Elizabeth Clark

Four diaries, each with silk-wrapped corners and covered in Japanese paper. 4" x 5 ¼" x ¼" (10 cm x 13.5 cm x .5 cm); wrapper: 4 ½" x 5 ⅜" x 1 ⅜" (11 cm x 13.5 cm x 4 cm)

Clark's diaries chronicle her adventures over the course of a year, with each diary containing the events of a season. The books all have Japanese bindings, but each is sewn a little differently. The wraparound case, called maru chitsu, is designed to hold several volumes.

3. HOMMAGE TO THE WAKING DREAM

Miriam Beerman

Mixed media, collage. 12" x 9 ½" (30 cm x 24 cm)

Abstract Expressionism was at its height when Beerman started as an artist, and its influence is readily apparent in her work. Her books function as journals, all of them an outlet for self-expression. When she paints and draws in her books, she follows only her intuition as opposed to planning what an image will look like. She says the mark-making process "stimulates and calms me. These marks are the equivalent of words—my language. They are the connecting link between the subconscious and the page."

1.

2.

1. JUBAL'S DIARY

Judy & Michael Jacobs

Mixed media. 9 1/4" x 5 3/4" x 5/8"
(23.5 cm x 14.5 cm x 1 cm)

Jubal's Diary is a science-fiction journal meant to be from the future, with
sketches of topography and vegetation
on a newly discovered planet. Both
books feature stub bindings and fit
into a hand-painted canvas belt pouch
so you can write as you go.

2. HOUSE BOOKS I-IV

Laurie Snyder

Cyanotype vertical accordion-fold books,
hardbound in cloth. 85" x 15" (216 cm x
38 cm) open; 14" x 15" (36 cm x 38 cm)
closed

Snyder's four hanging books deal with
the love of home and the emotions
brought on by a move. When folded,
the books open like a letter to create a
house form.

3. DREAMER DREAMING

Deborah Davidson

Handmade paper of flaxen cotton. 10 pages.
22" x 14" (56 cm x 36 cm)

This is one of several books Davidson
made in response to a series of narrative dreams she had about her father,
who had died long before. She and her
father are the two personae in this
book, which includes a poem she wrote
that begins: "My father is searching
through my dreams, through my psy-
che for himself. Myself. The dreams
are a journey. I am the conduit and the
recipient." The back of each of the
pages is a solid color that goes from
light to dark, alluding to the transition
from waking to the dream state.

4. REAL THINGS PEOPLE SAID AND I DIDN'T KNOW WHAT TO SAY

Thorsten Dennerline

Accordion-fold book with nine copper-plate
etchings on handmade paper, bound in
leather. 7" x 6" x 2" (18 cm x 15 cm x 5 cm)

Dennerline's book, which is meant to
be simultaneously critical and humorous, contains a selection of things
people really said that left the artist
flummoxed.

3.

1. DON'T BUG THE WAITRESS

Susan Baker

Folder with pockets, containing hand-silkscreened images on acid-free paper. 14" x 10" (36 cm x 25 cm)

All of Baker's books are autobiographical. In this book, the artist takes a humorous look at her experiences as a waitress.

2. HOWARDS & HOOVERS: A SAMPLE BOOK OF CHINESE-AMERICAN MALE NAMES

Indigo Som

Letterpress, watercolor, and laser-print fan book. 7" x 2" x 1 ¼" (18 cm x 5 cm x 3.5 cm)

Som uses her books to explore the eccentricities, mundane particulars, and cultures, as she puts it, of her many communities—Asian/Pacific Americans, women of color, and progressive activists, among others. She says she prefers humor and irony to dogma. In this book on Chinese-American first names, she examines community and identity in a very quiet but profound way.

3. LITTLE ORPHAN ANAGRAM

Susan Bee and Charles Bernstein

Mixed media. 11" x 8 ½" (28 cm x 22 cm)

This book, which features collages of original and found images, such as pictures from nineteenth- and early twentieth-century children's books, is a dreamlike interpretation of childhood.

1.

2.

1. DAILY PLANNER

Kez van Oudheusden

Painted silk-covered book with recycled
handmade paper and pigskin spine.
7" x 5" x 1" (18 cm x 13 cm x 3 cm)

Most people carry a Filofax as their
day planner, but Van Oudheusden has
made one of his own design that will
be saved as an artwork and a personal
archive.

2. PHOTO ALBUM WITH BOX

Elizabeth Clark

Suede-covered photo album with inset of
faux leopard fur; album is housed in a
cloth-covered clamshell box. Book:
5 1/8" x 5 1/8" x 3/8" (13 cm x 13 cm x 1 cm);
box: 6 1/4" x 5 1/4" x 1 1/4"
(16 cm x 13.5 cm x 4.5 cm)

Clark created this book to house
photographs she took of her friend
Sophie. The book's structure is a
modified accordion: The spine is a
mini-accordion, and Clark attached
the pages to the "valleys" of the folds.

3. BEGINNINGS

Kamal Boullata

Two-sided format with linocut.
8 3/4" x 4 1/2" (22.5 cm x 11 cm)

Boullata's book features a love poem in
English and Arabic by the Arab poet,
Adonis. Boullata, a well-known Pales-
tinian painter, scholar, and researcher,
also explores geometric patterning and
color in this book. As the pages open,
the colors change from cool hues like
blue to hot reds, oranges, and yellows.
The book's two-sided format lends
itself perfectly to the bilingual text.

4. DAY JOURNAL

Phil Sultz

Envelope of honeysuckle vine laced with
birch bark, with string-bound notebook
of mulberry rice paper. Envelope: 7" x 5"
(18 cm x 13 cm); notebook: 6" x 4 1/4"
(15 cm x 10.5 cm)

Sultz's journal fits neatly into a rustic
envelope, perfect for carrying it along
where the day takes him.

Family & Friends

You're entering familiar territory when it comes to memory books about the people in your life. Who hasn't filled an album with photos of the ones they love?

Start your memory book by organizing your photographs by subject. Then, think about what other kinds of items go with this subject. For a book on your grandmother, you could gather things that she used or that represent her, such as playbills from her favorite shows.

Finally, design your book to suit your subject. Cover that book on your grandmother, for instance, with a kind of lace similar to what she might have had at her house.

There's really no way to go wrong with this kind of memory book: The more personal and specific you get, the better the book is.

holding her body

Why don't you wear your dress always? I ask.

NICE SPOT

Evangeline

Sisters

BASED ON A PROJECT BY SHIREEN HOLMAN

In this book about her daughters, who artist Shireen Holman and her husband adopted from India when the girls were infants, Holman includes their passport covers and pictures, a fabric design from their infant clothes, Indian handmade paper, and scenes from their life growing up in the United States. The artist wanted to represent not just the specifics of their lives, though, but also to describe their relationship with one another. So, the front and back covers show the girls first facing away from each other and then reaching out to each other, symbolic of both sibling rivalry and closeness. Holman made *Sisters* from a reduction linocut print that she then folded into a book, to which she added pop-up sections and photographs. As an alternative to linocut printing, though, try painting a single large sheet of paper; creating an image on a computer, printing it out, and then having a giant color copy made of it; or even making a collage of handmade papers to fold into a book with added photographs.

What You Need

Newsprint

Tracing paper

Ruler

Bone folder

Linoleum

Transfer paper

Relief-printing inks

Baren

Ink knives

Drawing paper for sketches

Printing paper for the book

Pencils

Utility knife

Linoleum cutting tools

Black marker (with an ultra-fine point)

Brayers

Spoon

PVA glue

step-by-step

1. Making a mock-up of the book

Make a mock-up out of newsprint the same size as the final book. The mock-up should show where the folds will be. Fold the book in half, then in eighths. Then reverse fold and cut on top.

a.

b.

c.

d.

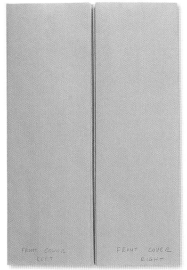

2. Marking pop-ups, photographs, and drawings

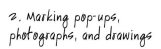

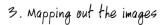

Clearly mark the exact location and size of the pop-ups, as well as the exact placement of the photographs, drawings, prints, and other images.

3. Mapping out the images

On tracing paper the size that the final linocut print will be, trace the images in the places they'll need to be in order to appear correctly when the print is folded into a book. Use transfer paper to transfer the drawings to the linoleum block. Go over the lines of the drawing with a permanent marker so it won't be erased after you print the first color. Then cut out the areas of the image to remain white in the final print so that they won't take any ink.

4. Printing the colors

Print the first stage yellow using oil-based relief inks. Roll the ink out onto a glass slab using a brayer. Then roll the ink onto the linoleum block and place the printing paper over the block. Place tracing paper over the printing paper so as not to damage it when transferring the image. Do the actual transfer with a baren and a spoon. Then cut the linoleum block some more, this time removing areas that you want to remain yellow, and print the second color red. Repeat this process, this time printing the final color, dark blue.

5. Folding the paper into a book

When the ink is dry, use a bone folder to crease the folds. Make the cuts necessary for the pop-ups and then paste the photographs in place using PVA glue.

Variation
MEMORIES OF MY FATHER

15" x 11" (38 cm x 28 cm)

Here, Holman made woodcuts and screen prints on handmade paper to once again combine the memories of two cultures. Her father immigrated to the United States from India, where he spent the last thirty years of his life (he died in 1994). *Memories of My Father* is in the form of one large book with several small booklets tucked into pockets. Like *Sisters,* this book also incorporates Indian handmade fabric designs.

Saquish

BASED ON A PROJECT BY CATHERINE BADOT-COSTELLO

Gaquish is a beach community in Plymouth, Massachusetts, where four generations of Catherine Badot-Costello's family have passed enjoyable times at their cottage. Over the years, many members of her family have been inspired by Saquish's marshes, sand dunes, rocky beach, and cozy bay to create art. So the artist decided to create a book of artwork by grandchildren in the family ranging in age from five to sixteen. Their art represents a few of their favorite things about visiting Saquish.

What You Need

Color copies of original artwork and photographs

Driftwood

Archival tape

Acid-free book board

Acid-free paper

PVA glue

Acrylic paint

Bone folder

step-by-step

1. Making the covers

First, cut two 11" x 13" (28 cm x 33 cm) pieces of book board to use as covers. To make a hinge for the book, trim 1 1/2" (4 cm) from the front cover at the spine edge, and then cut 1/2" (1 cm) from this trimmed piece. Assemble the front cover, gluing the 1/2" (1 cm) piece next to but not flush against the cover board on a strip of book cloth. Badot-Costello recommends gluing a strip of fabric to the front *and* back of the hinge on the front cover to reinforce it.

2. Making the pages

Next, cut pages slightly smaller than the book covers. Then, using the spine of the front cover as a guide, crease each page at the spine edge with a bone folder to provide ease of movement. Tip on (with small points of glue) strips of paper cut to the width of the spine to compensate for the thickness of the pages.

3. Mounting the artwork

Mark the placement of each piece of art-work and attach it to the page with a hinge made of archival tape. Put two points of glue at the bottom of the art-work to hold it in place if you don't want it to flip when the pages are turned.

4. Decorating the cover and binding the book

Cover the boards with Japanese paper painted with acrylic paint (Badot-Costello painted hers to look like sand) and bind the book using the Japanese side-sewn method. Etch or write in the title, and use a piece of driftwood as the closure.

Variation

LETTERS TO EVANGELINE

8 ½" x 5 ⅝" (22 cm x 14 cm)

To commemorate her grandmother Evangeline White's ninetieth birthday, Badot-Costello compiled letters written by White's five children and thirteen grandchildren describing their fondest memories of her. The letters were com-posed on a computer and laser-printed on archival paper. Since White was a gifted seamstress, one of her many quilts was color copied for the cover of the book, which was presented to her grandmother at her birthday party.

Emily & Spot

BASED ON A PROJECT BY RAYMOND H. STARR JR.

Raymond H. Starr Jr. was leafing through some snapshots he had taken of his granddaughter, Emily, when he decided that rather than frame the best pictures, he'd use them in a hand-made book. The artist chose seven images that, when arranged in a certain order, told the story of an encounter between a benign-looking but aggressive dog called Spot and a precocious child called Emily. Then he settled on a simple structure for his book: a Japanese stab binding with the boards covered in the same material as Emily's crib sheet. (Getting the material was harder than he expected: It had been discontinued, and he finally had to go straight to the manufacturer for a sheet of it.) The result: a memory book, complete with rubber stamps and photos, that looks at the world through his granddaughter's eyes.

What You Need

Newsprint

Handmade paper

Rubber stamps and ink pads

Book board

Book cloth

Photographs

Paste-paper photo corners

Spray fixative

Acrylic matte medium

Rabbitskin glue

PVA glue

Ruler

step-by-step

1. Making a dummy

Make a dummy for the text block out of newsprint to lay out the pictures and the text. Cut nine pieces of newsprint the size of an unfolded page 6 $^1/_2$" x 15" (17 cm x 38 cm), or the size of the available image area. (The actual pages will measure slightly larger, at 6 $^1/_2$" x 16 $^1/_2$" [17 cm x 42 cm], to allow for the binding.) Then map out the placement of the photos with a cardboard L-shaped template and note the placement of the text and rubber stamps on each page.

2. Making the covers

Cut book board slightly larger than the text block. Each cover will consist of two pieces of book board, one measuring 7 $^1/_2$" x 7 $^3/_4$" (19 cm x 19.5 cm) and another at 7 $^1/_2$" x $^3/_4$" (19 cm x 2 cm). (Use the smaller piece as the spine.) Then cut book cloth into a piece $^1/_2$" (1 cm) larger all around than the overall cover, making its dimensions 8 $^1/_2$" x 9 $^3/_4$" (22 cm x 24.5 cm). Coat the larger piece of book board with a 50/50 mixture of PVA glue and methyl cellulose, and place it on the book cloth so that there's a small margin of cloth on three sides of the board. Then coat the smaller piece of book board with the glue mixture and place it approximately $^1/_4$" (.5 cm) away from the larger piece of book board to form a hinge. Using a bone folder and additional glue, fold the fabric over the book board, repeating the entire process for the back cover. Decorate the inside of the covers with a paste-paper design.

3. Making the text block

To make lightweight paper more durable, coat it with a layer each of rabbitskin glue, acrylic matte medium, and spray fixative, in that order. Number each page on the spine edge, where it won't be visible when the book is bound, and, using the dummy as a guide, do all the rubber stamping. Finally, mount all of the photos on the appropriate pages using the same PVA-methyl cellulose mixture used on the covers.

4. Binding the book

Because Japanese stab binding does not include a conventional spine, the book will close flat, even with its two-dimensional pages. Or try an alternative binding such as metal posts used for accounting ledgers (available at office-supply stores). To accommodate material pasted onto the pages, simply insert several strips of paper between each page of the book at its spine—they will act as spacers for the pages.

Variation

MS. MANNERS'S GUIDE TO WATERMELON

3 ½" x 5 ½" x ¾" (9 cm x 14 cm x 2 cm)

Here again, Starr has turned snapshots of his granddaughter into a storybook—this time about her unique approach to dining on watermelon.

Family & Friends

1.

2.

3.

4.

1. DAYDREAMS FROM A
   SEASIDE RESPITE

KiP Walker

Mixed media, including cyanotype, beads,
thread, Japanese paper. 2 ¼" x 2 ¼"
(5 cm x 5 cm)

When she vacations with family at the
Carolina shore, Walker likes to bring
along an art project to do with her
nieces and young cousins. This book,
which includes wire, doilies, sand and
other found objects, was made from
one such visit.

2. MARGARET JANE PASSES ON:
   A DECLAMATION OF LIFE IN
   5 ACTS

KiP Walker

A framed book for hanging, consisting of
mixed media, including cyanotype, watercolor,
and found objects. 25" x 19" (64 cm x 48 cm)

Walker's book reflects on her mother's
life and what she passed on, as well as
her death. Her life is described in
stages: Child, Lover/Widow, Mother,
Teacher, and The Final Passing. The
book started with the artist's notion
that the common phrase "she passed
on" encompasses much more than just
a person's death. Her book includes
contributions by other family members, as well.

3. THE HANDS THAT HOLD ME

Emily Martin

Variation on coptic binding, with Japanese
and English book papers. 8" x 4" x 2"
(20 cm x 10 cm x 5 cm)

Martin often makes what she calls
collection books. She gathers together
a group of people, traces their hands,
and uses the tracings in a book.
Alternatively, she might make a book
of items collected from a certain location in order to maintain a sense of
the place. *The Hands That Hold Me*
contains tracings of the hands of
seventeen members of her family.

4. OLD WIFE'S TALE

Peter Madden

Handmade paper, solvent transfers, mixed-
media accordion-fold book. 7" x 12'
(18 cm x 366 cm)

This book spans Madden's grandmother's entire life. The text was written by the artist's grandparents, Marie
and William Sidley, whose presence is
a tangible part of the book. The cro-
cheting at either end of the book was
done by Madden's grandmother at the
turn of the century, and the beads that
hold the book shut were all restrung
from her necklaces and earrings.

1.

2.

3.

4.

1 . LULLABY FOR KENDRA

Susan Kapuscinski Gaylord

Mixed media, including color photocopies, gold marker, colored pencil, and Japanese paper. 10" x 13" (25 cm x 33 cm)

On a visit to the Children's Museum in Boston, the artist and her three-year-old daughter spent a lot of time in a little room where the familiar lullaby, "Mockingbird" ("Hush little baby, don't say a word. Papa's gonna buy you a mockingbird..."), played over and over. There was a display case containing all the objects mentioned in the song. The artist made a book of the song for her daughter, Kendra, changing papa to mama and collecting pictures from catalogs and magazines to represent each of the objects.

2 . A PURPLE DRESS

Kerrie Carbary

Accordion-fold stuffed fabric book, with relief prints and photocopies held together with purple ties. 6" x 4 1/2"; folds out to 9' (15 cm x 11 cm; folds out to 274 cm)

Carbary's mother made this dress, a housedress of sorts, when the artist was a child. Carbary says she always wanted a dress just like it, but she and her mom never got around to making it. The artist thinks of this purple dress as a symbol of her mother's spirit and her life.

3 . KAPUSCINSKI FAMILY BOOK

Susan Kapuscinski Gaylord

Laser-printed text, black-and-white and color photocopies, photographs, maps, rubber stamps, and gold Chinese spirit paper. 10 1/2" x 8 1/2" (27 cm x 22 cm)

The artist made this book as an example for a project on family history books. It concisely relates the story of her family, starting with her grandparents' arrival in America and ending with the birth of her son.

4 . LIFE-SENSE/LICENSE

Louise Neaderland

Twelve board pages, duotone black and brown photocopies. 10 2/3" x 6" x 7/8" (27 cm x 15 cm x 3 cm)

Neaderland's book follows the life of her father, starting when he first got his driver's license, depicting its growing importance to him (particularly when he had a family), and how he refused to give it up even when he was no longer capable of driving a car.

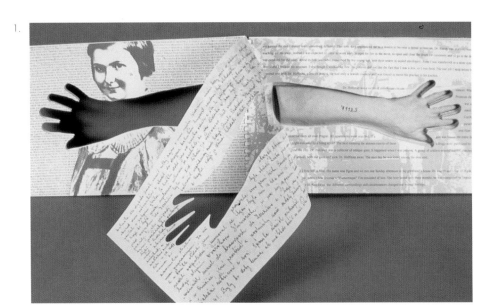

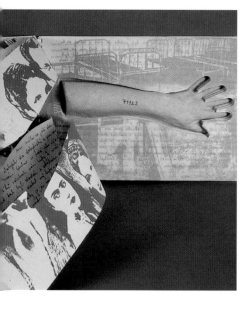

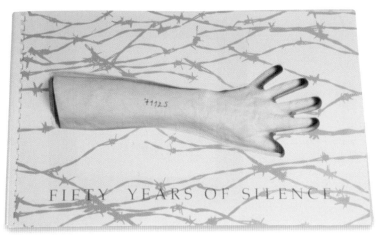

4.

1. 71125: FIFTY YEARS OF SILENCE

Tatana Kellner

Mixed media, including photographs, die-cut pages, and a handmade paper cast, all housed in a wooden box. 12" x 20" x 3" (30 cm x 51 cm x 8 cm)

Kellner's book details her parents' memories of internment in several concentration and extermination camps during World War II. She translated her parents' handwritten Czechoslovakian text into English (the original manuscript is reproduced on transparent interleaved pages). The pages fall around a plaster cast of her mother's arm, which bears the tattooed number she was given in the camps.

2. ALBUM

David Schlater

Computer laser printouts, photographs, and color copies. 12 1/2" x 9 1/2" (32 cm x 24 cm)

The artist got the inspiration to create *Album* when he inherited a stack of deteriorating photos and memento albums, which spanned half a century, from his grandmother. These albums documented her life from when she was a young child, to her dating and high school experiences, to her first marriage, to her husband's death. Schlater, who had never known his grandfather, chose to reproduce some of these materials and make his own album, one that would better stand the test of time—and that presented his new acquaintance with this mysterious member of his family.

3. UNTITLED GIFT BOOK

Mindell Dubansky

Felt pages and linen cover, with cotton embroidery floss, shell buttons, and pearl beads. 6 3/4" x 6" x 1" (17.5 cm x 15 cm x 3 cm)

Dubansky made this book for her mother, who is fond of sewing. The book is based on traditional nine-teenth-century needle books made with felt pages that women used to store their collection of sewing needles or pins.

4. FRAGMENTS FROM THE PAST

Evelyn Eller

Mixed media, including color photocopies, monoprints, collage, and Oriental papers. 10 1/6" x 12 1/2" (25 cm x 32 cm)

When this book is standing up, its pages fold out like a sail, making this a sculpture as much as a book. The book visually chronicles Eller's parents' lives when they were young, including their engagement and wedding pictures.

1.

2.

3.

4.

1. MILESTONES

Evelyn Eller

Mixed media, including a cigar box, Indian and Japanese papers, and photocopies. 8" x 8" x 1" (20 cm x 20 cm x 3 cm)

Each page of this book represents a highlight in the artist's life, including her graduation from college, her wedding, and the birth of her children.

2. MARBLE BOX

Elizabeth Clark

Binder's board with Moriki (Japanese paper), bone clasp, hinge whittled from a chopstick, glass-covered opening, and 45 glass marbles. 4 5/8" x 4" x 4 1/8" (11 cm x 10 cm x 10 cm)

Each of the forty-five marbles in Clark's treasure box represents a day in the six weeks she spent visiting with a close friend of hers from Thailand.

3. TRANSMUTATION

Lois Polansky

Mixed-media accordion-fold book with hand-made paper. 16 1/2" x 62" (42 cm x 157 cm)

Part of a series Polansky did on her family, *Transmutation* is an extremely personal book about the artist's mother, and the technique behind it is very much related to the subject matter. The book features prints by Polansky, except instead of preserving the plate between printings, she changed it each time. After many printings, nearly all the details of the image were removed from the plate except for the silhouette. Not long after she finished this book, her mother became seriously ill, making the fading images of *Transmutation* a haunting suggestion of what was to come.

4. SOME OF MY MOTHER'S THINGS

Laurie Snyder

Eighteen silver prints, dry-mounted on Mohawk paper, one platinum 4 x 5 photograph, hardbound in linen and cyanotype, Florentine endpapers. 14" x 28" (36 cm x 71 cm) open; 14" x 14" (36 cm x 36 cm) closed

Snyder's book documents and celebrates her mother's home (the artist's childhood home). She photographed collections of her mother's things, such as a desk drawer of eyeglasses, boxes of keys, boxes of letters, music stands, her bathrobe, her garden, and so on. The sequence of photographs make what Snyder calls an homage portrait.

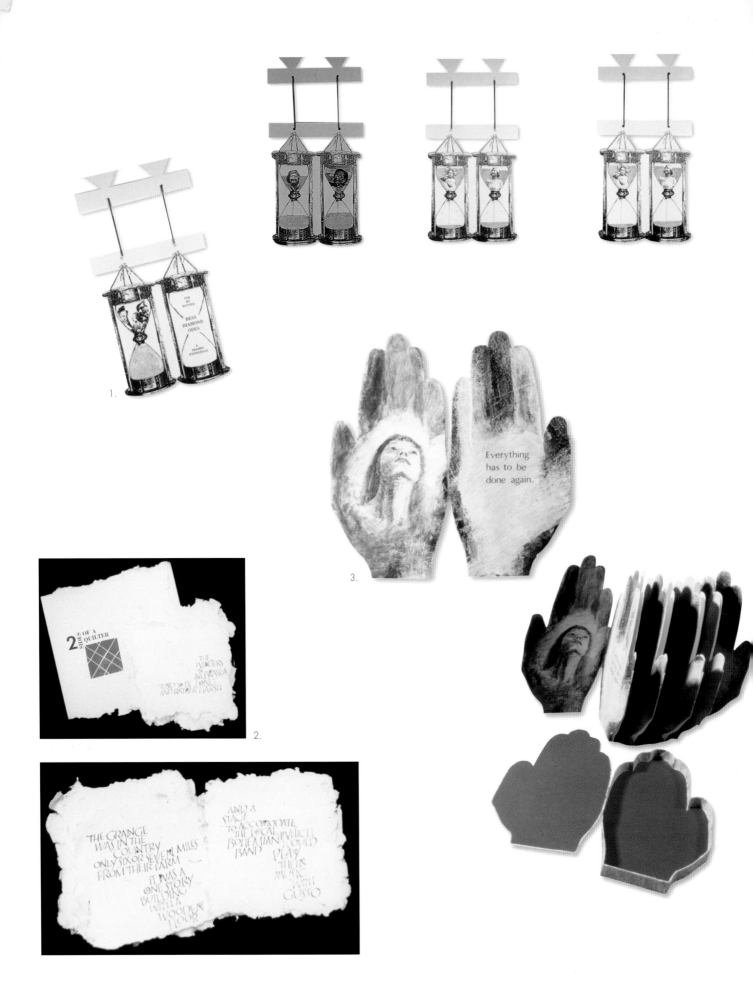

4.

1. OUR GLASS

Louise Neaderland

Seven hand-cut pages with real sand that filters to the bottom of the last page as the pages are turned. 7" x 10" (18 cm x 25 cm)

Here the artist depicts her mother's life, from young girl to old woman, with the sand starting at the top of the hourglass and filtering to the bottom as the pages (which are similar to calendar pages, another reference to time) are turned. This book is part of Neaderland's series, "Where Is Home?," about her parents, the passage of time, and the endurance of sand. The books were made over a period of about four years when both her parents were in nursing homes, a traumatic time for the artist and her sister.

2. 2 SIDES OF A QUILTER

Pamela Paulsrud

Unbound, with calligraphy, letterpress, linoleum block, and cyanotype prints on handmade paper. Cover: 7" x 7 1/2" (18 cm x 19 cm); pages: 5" x 5" (13 cm x 13 cm)

Paulsrud's mother wrote the text for this book about Paulsrud's grandmother, a quilter who also liked to go dancing. The title derives from the artist's desire to show another side of her grandmother. So many books have been written about quilters and quilting, she says, but a quilt has more than one side—and so do those who make them.

3. UNTITLED HANDBOOK WITH PREDICTION

Crystal Cawley

Mixed media, including handmade Japanese paper, acrylics, ink, and rub-on type; with handmade box. 7" x 4" (18 cm x 10 cm)

Cawley, who says she has an obsession with hand shapes, made this book at a time in her life when a friend of hers was fighting a losing battle with a fatal illness. The striking images in this book were influenced by ones she saw on billboards while traveling in Paris and Prague.

4. AT GRANDMOTHER'S HOUSE

Kerrie Carbary

Accordion-fold book, with hand-printed etchings and hand-lettered text. 6" x 6" (15 cm x 15 cm)

Carbary's book features her own text about her relationship with her grandmother, touching on shared heritage, the television as babysitter, and aging.

special events

Making a memory book about the important events in life
is a way to both relive the experience and marvel at all that
went into it.

Let's say you were planning a family reunion. You could
make a memory book that would include old family photos
and new pictures from the reunion. You could even get
everyone else to contribute something, whether it be an
anecdote or pictures from their own life. When it was done,
the book would be a family chronicle.

There are so many times in life that are turning points, and
then plenty that are simply notable side roads. In either case,
they all go by so fast, and some of them we would like to
revisit at our own pace. Memory books make that possible.

Mini Wedding Book

BASED ON A PROJECT BY STEPHANIE LATER

Artist Stephanie Later started making wedding books as gifts; they were an engaging means of encompassing everything that leads up to a wedding—from cards and telegrams to party favors from the shower and engagement party. She is especially fond of the accordion-fold wedding book because it can be filled with favorite photographs and mementos, and displayed at home, as you would a framed picture. Plus, it's easy to take with you on those visits to family members who may have missed the big event.

What You Need

Book cloth

Decorative lace, embroidered items (linens from flea markets, old clothing, etc.)

PVA glue

Bone folder

Ruler

Utility knife

Cutting surface

Archival binder's board

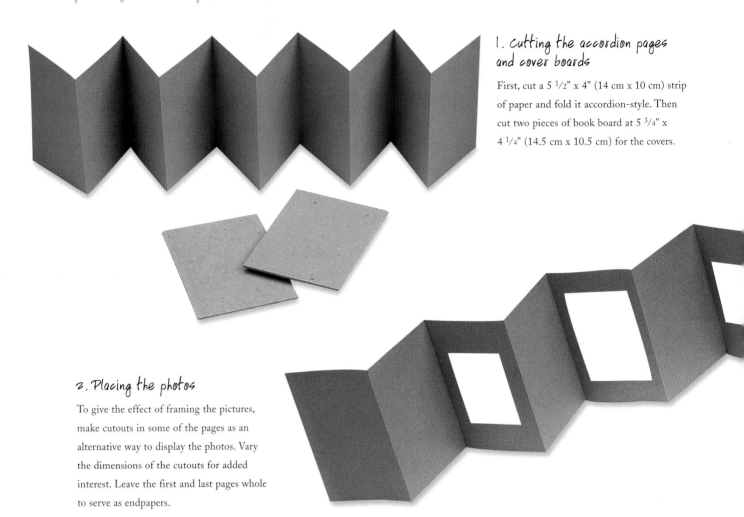

1. Cutting the accordion pages and cover boards

First, cut a 5 ½" x 4" (14 cm x 10 cm) strip of paper and fold it accordion-style. Then cut two pieces of book board at 5 ¾" x 4 ¼" (14.5 cm x 10.5 cm) for the covers.

2. Placing the photos

To give the effect of framing the pictures, make cutouts in some of the pages as an alternative way to display the photos. Vary the dimensions of the cutouts for added interest. Leave the first and last pages whole to serve as endpapers.

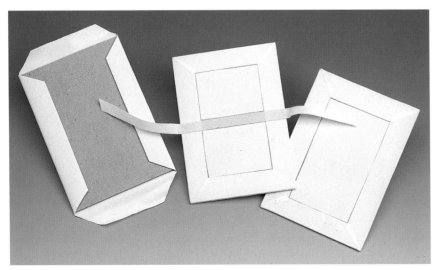

3. Making the covers

Glue the cover boards onto the fabric and trim the edges. Then glue a piece of ribbon across the inside center of the bottom cover to serve as the closure for the book. Cover the exposed book board with extra fabric.

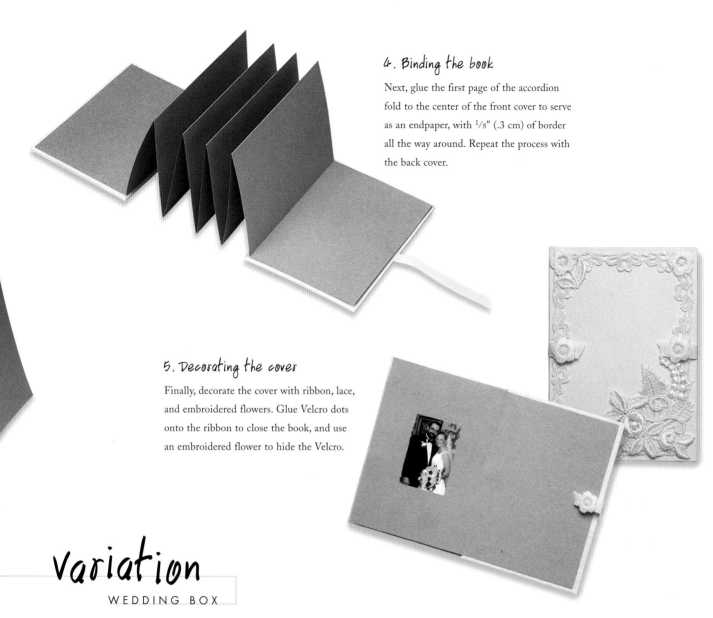

4. Binding the book

Next, glue the first page of the accordion fold to the center of the front cover to serve as an endpaper, with $1/8"$ (.3 cm) of border all the way around. Repeat the process with the back cover.

5. Decorating the cover

Finally, decorate the cover with ribbon, lace, and embroidered flowers. Glue Velcro dots onto the ribbon to close the book, and use an embroidered flower to hide the Velcro.

Variation

WEDDING BOX

13 ¾" x 9 ¾" (35 cm x 24.5 cm)

Later created this wedding box to house keepsakes such as the wedding garter, dried flowers, and a piece of the bride's veil. (Later, who has worked as a conservator at the Metropolitan Museum of Art in New York City, emphasizes the importance of using archival materials for boxes and books so they will stand the test of time.) She lined the box with beautiful handmade paper with flowers pressed into it. Or, to make it more personal, she'll write a love poem around the border in gold pen.

Wedding Photo Album

*R*aven Regan enjoys making this style of book because it can be customized for any purpose. It measures 9" x 11 ¹/₄" (23 cm x 28.5 cm), so standard 8 ¹/₂" x 11" (22 cm x 28 cm) paper fits perfectly inside. The weight of the pages can vary from a quality bond for a guest book, to a card stock for a photo album, to handmade paper for a gardener's journal. The covers are equally versatile, with papers, ribbons, or patterns used as decoration. Regan personalizes her wedding books by using colors and ribbons she knows the bride likes and by including an invitation to the wedding on the cover—and perhaps even using a quotation of significance to the couple.

What You Need

Two pieces decorative cover paper measuring 10 ¹/₂" x 11" (27 cm x 28 cm) each

Two pieces binding cloth measuring 11" x 5" (28 cm x 13 cm) each

Two pieces endpaper measuring 9 ¹/₈" x 8 ¹/₂" (23 cm x 22 cm) each

Two pieces Mill board measuring 9" x 11" (23 cm x 28 cm)

29 pages measuring 8 ¹/₂" x 11" (22 cm x 28 cm)

Ribbon

PVA glue

29 pages gold-stamped vellum paper

Scissors

Utility knife

Clamps

1" (3 cm) foam glue brush

Drill

Bone folder

Large-eye needle

Glue stick

Metal ruler

Pencil

Decorations for cover: gold no-hole beads, glitter, and charms

Gold photo corners

Gold marker

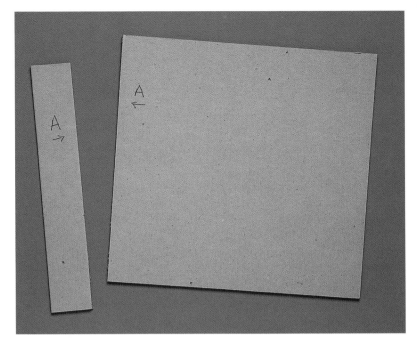

1. Cutting the covers

Cut two pieces of Mill board to 9" x 11" (23 cm, x 28 cm), and then cut a 9" x 1 ¹/₂" (23 cm x 4 cm) strip from each of these cover boards. Use the smaller strips for the spine.

2. Covering the boards

Thin some PVA glue with water, making it the consistency of coffee cream. Then use a 1" (3 cm) sponge brush to apply the glue to the back of each cover board and adhere them to the inside of the decorative paper. Make the boards flush on the binding side (the left side) and centered, with equal margins of paper on the other three sides. Then fold the cloth over and turn the two corners in at a 45-degree angle; glue the paper to the board. Finally, glue the endpapers to each board.

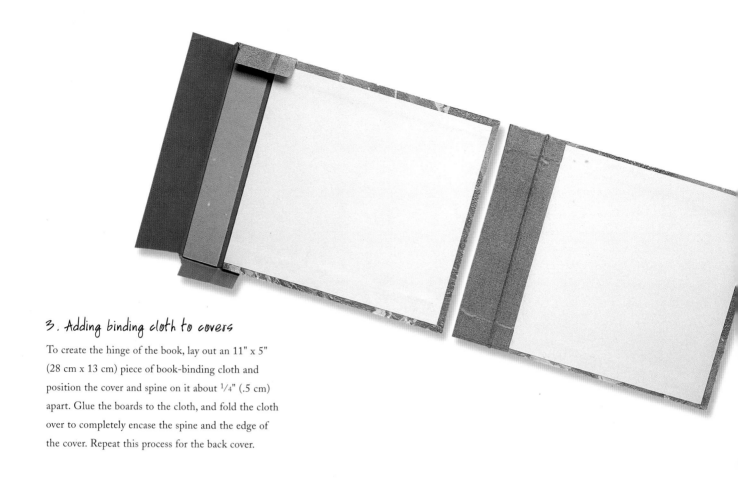

3. Adding binding cloth to covers

To create the hinge of the book, lay out an 11" x 5"
(28 cm x 13 cm) piece of book-binding cloth and
position the cover and spine on it about $1/4$" (.5 cm)
apart. Glue the boards to the cloth, and fold the cloth
over to completely encase the spine and the edge of
the cover. Repeat this process for the back cover.

4. Making the pages

To make the pages fold back easily, score each one
$1 3/4$" (4.5 cm) in from the left at the spine with a
bone folder. If necessary, add spacers at the spine
measuring $8 1/2$" x $1 1/2$" (22 cm x 4 cm) cut from
the same paper as the pages.

5. Binding the book

To use a Japanese side-sewn binding, as Regan did here, mark and drill five holes along the spine (through the cover boards, pages, and spacers, which you should clamp together to keep them from moving). Make the end holes 1" (3 cm) in from the top and bottom (or head and tail) of the book. The other holes should be 1 3/4" (4.5 cm) apart. Indent all the holes 3/4" (2 cm) from the binding edge, then sew the book together with ribbon.

6. Decorating the cover and pages

Embellish the decorative-paper cover with cut-out hearts, ribbon, gold photo corners, and charms. For the inside, add photos with gold photo corners and text written in gold marker.

Variation

MATRIMONY MOMENTS

9" x 11 ¼" (23 cm x 28.5 cm)

To make a different book using the same structure and binding, add a framed wedding photo to the cover and embellish it with braided ribbon and a heart locket.

Home Design Folio

BASED ON A PROJECT BY DEBORAH WAIMON

Waimon's *Home Renovation Folio* can serve two functions. You can take it with you as you make the rounds to paint stores, furniture showrooms, antique shops, and anywhere else your renovation plans may take you. Use it to collect business cards, paint chips, and fabric swatches. Or, you can use the book as a means of documenting the actual renovation of the house, filling it with photos of the house in progress. For this artist, the practicality of this folio structure is exactly what makes it appealing.

What You Need

Book board

Book cloth

Heavyweight thread

PVA glue

A couple of sheets of medium- to heavyweight paper

¼" (.5 cm) ribbon

½" (1 cm) ribbon

Needle

Bone folder

Utility knife

step-by-step

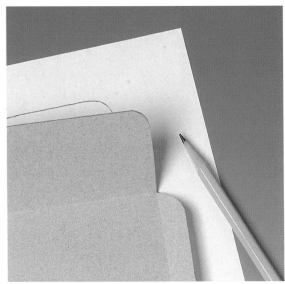

1. Making the envelopes

Make an envelope pattern by opening an existing envelope and using it as a template. The envelope used here is 4" (10 cm) wide and 5" (13 cm) long, but any size can be used. Trace the pattern onto the paper you have chosen, then cut out five envelopes, score along the fold lines, and fold into shape (do not glue together yet!).

2. Making the spine

To make the accordion spine, cut a piece of paper $^1/_4$" (.5 cm) wider than the folded envelope—here 4" (10 cm)—and twice the length of the envelope—here 14 $^1/_2$" (37 cm)—plus 4 $^1/_2$" (11 cm). To create folds in the accordion spine, measure 5 $^1/_8$" (13 cm) down from the top—this is the length of the folded envelope plus $^1/_8$" (.3 cm)—make a score line and make the first fold. Continue scoring and folding at $^1/_2$" (1 cm) increments until there are nine folds and five "valley" folds.

3. Adding the envelopes to the spine

Next, put a scored and folded (but unglued) envelope into the valley of the spine and clip it with clothespins. Measure $3/4$" (2 cm) in from each side of the spine as shown; make a row of seven equally spaced pencil marks in the valley, then poke each mark gently through with a needle. Repeat with all the valley folds.

4. Attaching the envelopes

To begin sewing, cut an 8" (20 cm) length of thread (this is twice the width of the envelope) and sew the bottom of the envelope to the spine, as shown. Leave a 3" (8 cm) "tail" of thread. Sew all six stitches across and back, meeting up with the tail. Tie the ends together with a double knot and dot it with glue.

After each envelope has been stitched, glue the seams together (but don't glue the opening!).

5. Binding, (part 1)

Cut two pieces of narrow ribbon approximately 5" (13 cm) long. Turn the folio upside down and slip the end of the ribbon through the first stitch of each "mountain fold." Repeat this process with the second piece of ribbon on the last row of stitches. (If the ribbon begins to fray, try adding a small piece of tape to the end till you are finished.)

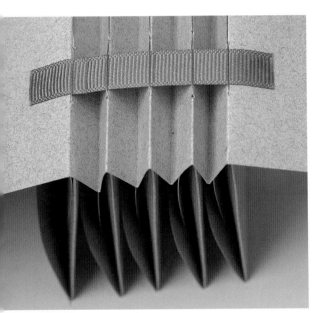

6. Binding, (part 2)

Adjust the tension of the accordion folds—you can pull them tightly together or leave the arrangement very loose, depending on how many items you plan to store in each envelope. Glue the ribbon tabs to the outside of the spine (here each tab is about $1/2$" [1 cm] of ribbon).

7. Making the covers

Cut two pieces of book board 4 $1/2$" (11 cm) wide and 5 $1/4$" (13.5 cm) long. (This is $1/2$" [1 cm] wider than the width of an envelope and $1/4$" [.5 cm] longer.) Cover the book boards with book cloth (decorative paper can also be used), and decorate the cover with a collage related to the project. Glue the wider ribbon underneath the collage to use as a tie closure for the folio.

8. Merging the folio and the covers

Glue the accordion folio to the uncovered sides of the book board, being careful to center it. Weight down the covers with a heavy object while the glue dries.

Variation

GARDEN FOLIO

5 ½" x 4 ½" (14 cm x 11 cm)

Waimon's envelope folios are endlessly adaptable. Here she used the format to create a garden book for keeping seed packets, before-and-after photos, and notes regarding the planning and planting of a garden. The book can also be used to store dried flowers. Waimon's collaged cover incorporates actual leaves and pictures of flowers in lieu of a title to suggest the contents.

Special Events

A GALLERY OF BOOKS

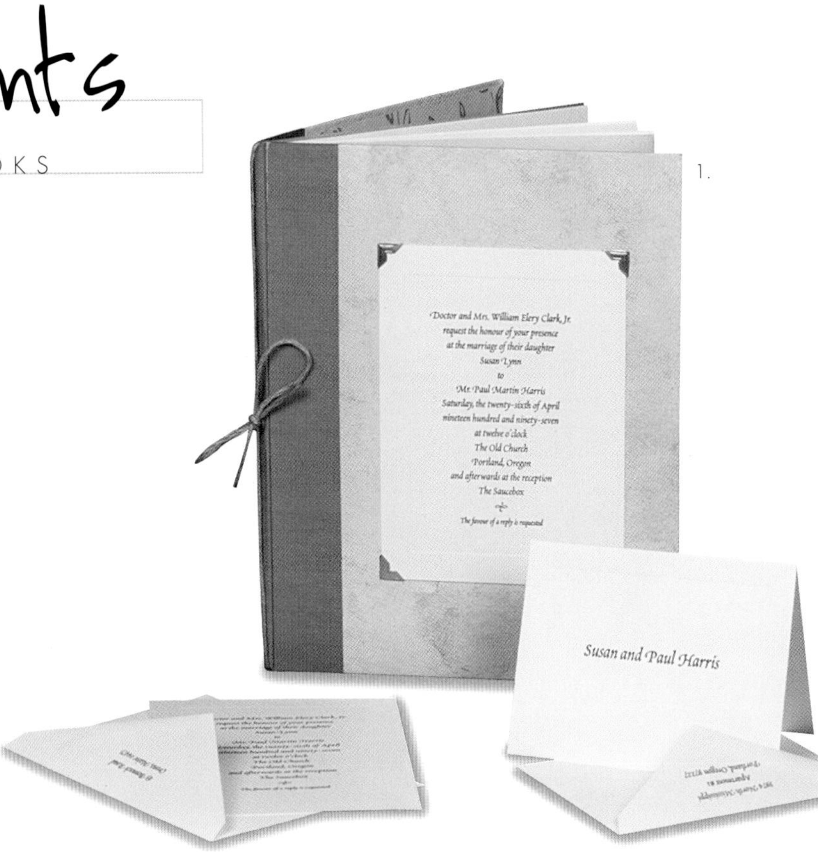

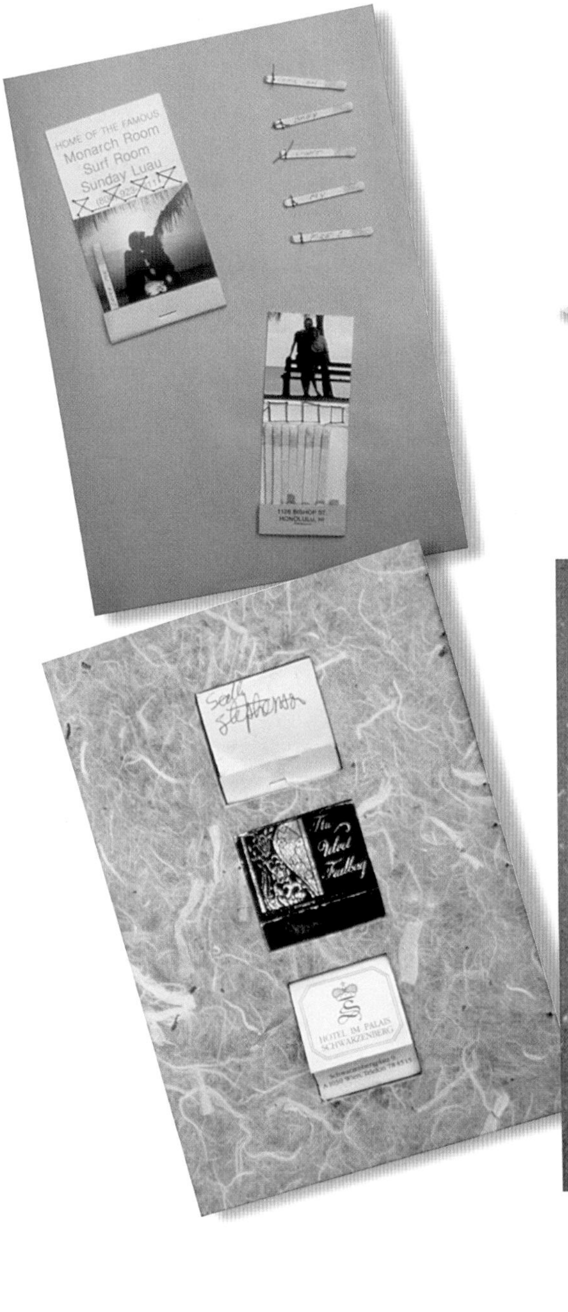

Doctor and Mrs. William Elery Clark, Jr.
request the honour of your presence
at the marriage of their daughter
Susan Lynn
to
Mr. Paul Martin Harris
Saturday, the twenty-sixth of April
nineteen hundred and ninety-seven
at twelve o'clock
The Old Church
Portland, Oregon
and afterwards at the reception
The Saucebox
The favour of a reply is requested
Susan and Paul Harris
1.

HOME OF THE FAMOUS
Monarch Room
Surf Room
Sunday Luau
HOTEL IM PALAIS
SCHWARZENBERG

The Art of Marriage
183
Marriage
Manual
2.

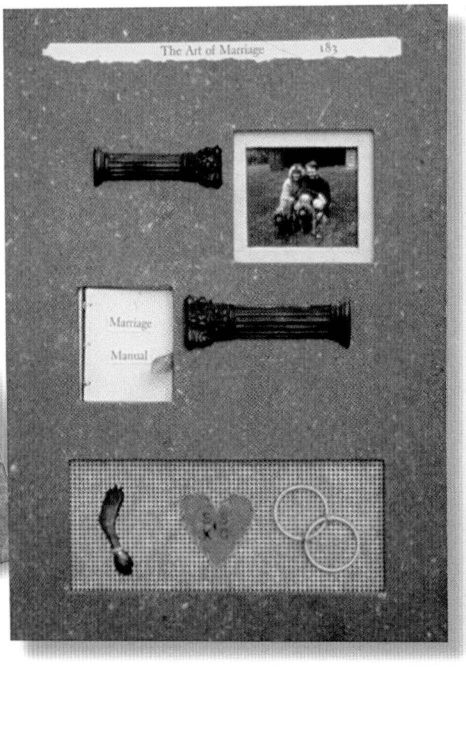

3.

1. WEDDING ALBUM

Elizabeth Clark

Hand-letterpress printed wedding invitations, stationery, and wedding album. 12" x 9 ³/₄" x ³/₈" (30 cm x 24.5 cm x 1 cm)

This album, which Clark made for her sister as a wedding gift, features a cover made from Mexican Bark paper and silk book cloth.

2. THE ART OF MARRIAGE (ANNIVERSARY BOOK)

Joan Soppe

Mixed media, including machine- and hand-made paper, letterpress, and matchbooks. 12" x 7" x 4" (30 cm x 18 cm x 10 cm)

Soppe created this book for a client who presented it to her husband on their tenth anniversary. The woman had saved all manner of mementos from her marriage, including the matchbook in which her future husband had written his phone number when they met and a matchbook from their honeymoon in Switzerland. The client gave Soppe complete freedom to do with the keepsakes what she would. Soppe even etched onto copper plates the blueprints to a new home the couple was building.

3. BIRD STORIES

Mary Ann Sampson

Mixed media, including Alpha rag board, Prisma pencils, acrylics, and wood
Barn, 12" x 11 ¹/₂" x 6 ¹/₄" (30 cm x 29 cm x 16 cm); book, 6 ¹/₂" x 6" (17 cm x 15 cm)

Sampson and her husband built a barn in the late 1980s that became a recurring theme in her books. *Bird Stories* is a beak-shaped book that celebrates the barn's first residents.

4.

1. KENDRA'S BIRTHDAY BOOK

Susan Kapuscinski Gaylord

Accordion-fold book, with Canson Mi-Teintes paper. 8 ½" x 5" (22 cm x 13 cm)

The artist's daughter turned five just after Gaylord got a new Mac with a scanner and color printer. This book was the first project made with her new equipment. Gaylord made a page for each year of Kendra's life, each with a four-line rhyming verse, the year, a flap with the number, and a photo under the flap.

2. KENDRA'S DAY

Susan Kapuscinski Gaylord

Mixed media, including mat board, contact paper, ribbon, and photos. 8 ½" x 6 ½" (22 cm x 17 cm)

For this book celebrating her daughter Kendra's second birthday, the artist photographed the child throughout her day (at breakfast, riding in her stroller, having ice cream, etc.). The colorful circles that decorate the border are like Cheerios, which is what her daughter had for breakfast that day.

3. WINTER LIGHT

Peter Sramek and Hannah Tillich

Blue silk binding, Oasis leather spine on raised cords, 13 photographic etchings, and letterpress. 9" x 8 ½" (23 cm x 22 cm)

Hannah Tillich composed the poem for this book, which she and artist Peter Sramek made when Tillich's husband, the theologian Paul Tillich, died. The photos—abstract images of frost or rain on windows and several landscapes—are all by Sramek.

4. MULE DAY PARADE

Mary Ann Sampson

Mixed media, including watercolor paper, photocopies, ink, intaglio prints, and handmade French paper. 8 ¼" x 6 ¼" (21 cm x 16 cm)

The Mule Day Parade in Benson, North Carolina, was an annual event that took place at harvest time. Sampson, who was a majorette for her school at the time, participated in the event with the school band. This book, which was inspired by her experience, has pages that form pockets containing pull-out characters who can be positioned around the book.

1.

2.

3.

1. IN THE LIGHT OF PASSING

Peter Sramek

Mixed media, including photocollages, Rives BFK paper, and colored pencils. 14 ³/₄" x 11 ¹/₂" (37.5 cm x 29 cm)

Sramek produced this book in response to the death of his uncle. The text is a poem written in four stanzas that appears through cutouts in the pages. The pages are folded in thirds and fold out to full length on viewing, and the cutouts layer and reconfigure the lines as the pages are turned.

2. MEMORIAL BOOK

Nora Lockshin, Patricia Blair Ryan, and Julia Kushnirsky

Cover of three different handmade papers with grass, leaf, and fiber inclusions; single sheets were side-sewn with green linen thread. 9" x 8" (23 cm x 20 cm)

Lockshin hand-bound this collection of essays, poems, photographs, and memoirs written by friends of the book's subject, Jim Secundy, and collected by Ryan. Kushnirsky designed the book, which was created through the wonders of desktop publishing (QuarkXPress for the text with sepia Fiery prints and labels). Despite the technology behind the book, its rustic aesthetic evokes Secundy's personal commitment to the environment and his respect for nature.

3. MARRIAGE VOWS

Evelyn Eller

Mixed media, including color photocopies and linen paper. 11 ¹/₄" x 12 ¹/₄" (28.5. cm x 31 cm)

Eller made this book as a wedding gift for her daughter.

1.

2.

3.

1. I MISS MY HOUSE BOOK

Laurie Snyder

Twenty pages, nine double-spread cyanotype and paste-paper monoprints, machine-sewn fore edges, with hardcover quarter binding in handmade paper and linen with cyanotype title inset. 22" x 15" (56 cm x 38 cm) closed; 22" x 30" (56 cm x 76 cm) open

Snyder made this book after she moved to Baltimore from Ithaca, New York, to take a teaching job. Rather than documenting the actual move, she responded visually to the loss of her family, the change in the family structure when the children grow up and move out, and the dramatic shift from a rural to an urban lifestyle.

2. THE BIOLOGY OF MARRIAGE (WEDDING BOOK)

Joan Soppe

Mixed media. 5 ½" x 3 ½" (14 cm x 9 cm)

For this wedding book, which was made on commission, Soppe incorporated some of the couple's mementos, such as their wedding announcement from the newspaper, with her own clippings from an old book on marriage. She left some of the pages blank so the couple could add their own text.

3. RECOLLECTIONS

Pamela Paulsrud

Accordion-fold book with mixed media, including cyanotype and watercolor paper. 4" x 3" (10 cm x 8 cm)

Paulsrud made this book for her daughter for her high school graduation. She scanned images of her daughter dating from when she was a baby up to the present and manipulated them in Photoshop. She then had negatives of these images made at a service bureau and printed them with cyanotype on watercolor paper, where she further manipulated them with oils and Prismacolors.

1. HOME DREAMS

Carol Barton

Accordion-fold book with pop-ups.
6" x 4" (15 cm x 10 cm) closed

Barton's book was inspired by the renovation of her house, an ongoing project. While planning for the renovation, she kept notes of things she would like to include in her dream house, along with ideas that other people had for their own dream homes. The text is derived from these notions of a dream house.

2. THE HABITAT

Pamela Paulsrud

Unbound book with wooden box; corrugated paper, dirt, thorns, and grapevines. Box: 5" (13 cm) square

The pages of this unbound book are lifted out of the box with a small purple ribbon. The text, by the artist, recalls an episode from a summer visit with her grandparents. Her grandfather had built a habitat—an enclosure of trees and plants that serves as a haven for small animals—in the backyard during the Depression. Paulsrud and her brother, with their grandmother, would occasionally break through the perimeter to pick plums from trees growing inside the habitat. She says the habitat would open like magic on these outings. Years later, when her grandmother died, Paulsrud and her brother returned to the habitat and attempted to break through to find the plums that lay inside—but now the habitat was impenetrable.

contributors

Jody Alexander
195 Adams Street
Newton, MA 02158

Catherine Badot-Costello
20 Purchase Street
Newburyport, MA 01950

Susan Baker
Box 163
North Truro, MA 02652

Carol Barton
6005 Yale Avenue
Glen Echo, MD 20812

Laura Blacklow
215 Erie Street
Cambridge, MA 02139

Susan Bee and Charles Bernstein
215 W. 92nd Street, #5F
New York, NY 10025

Miriam Beerman
6 Macopin Avenue
Montclair, NJ 07043

Kamal Boullata
c/o Pyramid Atlantic
6001 66th Avenue, Suite 103
Riverdale, MD 20737

Kerrie Carbary
2244 NW 62nd Street
Seattle, WA 98107

Crystal Cawley
142 High Street, Suite 223
Portland, ME 04101

Elizabeth Clark
8530 N. 22nd Avenue, Apt. 1042
Phoenix, AZ 85021

Jane Conneen
The Little Farm Press,
820 Andrews Road
Bath, PA 18014

Béatrice Coron
372 Central Park West, Apt. 20D
New York, NY 10025

Carolynn Dallaire
189-65 B Street
Delta, BC, Canada
V4L 1M9

Deborah Davidson
1 Fitchburg Street
Somerville, MA 02143

Donna Marie deCreeft
241 W. 20th Street
New York, NY 10011

Thorsten Dennerline
211 S. Pleasant Street
Amherst, MA 01002

Mindell Dubansky
c/o Metropolitan Museum of Art
1000 Fifth Avenue
New York, NY 10028-0198

Joan Duff-Bohrer
123 Gillis Hill Lane
Salem, NY 12865

Evelyn Eller
71-49 Harrow Street
Forest Hills, NY 11375-5957

Susan Kapuscinski Gaylord
Box 852
Newburyport, MA 01950

Lonnie Graham
c/o Pyramid Atlantic
6001 66th Avenue, Suite 103
Riverdale, MD 20737

Sandy Groebner
79 Belsize Drive
Toronto, Ontario, Canada
M4S 1L3

Barbara Harman
3316 Harriet Avenue South
Minneapolis, MN 55408-3728

Susan Hensel
6077 Horizon Drive
East Lansing, MI 48823

Shireen Holman
c/o Pyramid Atlantic
6001 66th Avenue, Suite 103
Riverdale, MD 20737

Mei-Ling Hom
2306 Fitzwater Street
Philadelphia, PA 19146

Judy and Michael Jacobs
P.O. Box 19458
Seattle, WA 98109-1458

Tatana Kellner
552 Binnewater Road
Kingston, NY 12401

Ann Kresge
200 Mossybrook Road
High Falls, NY 12440

Stephanie Later
201 E. 77th Street
New York, NY 10021

Edna Lazaron
7711 Argyle Avenue
Norfolk, VA 23505

Nora Lockshin
c/o Lance
628 E. 20th Street., Apt. 5B,
New York, NY 10009

Peter Madden
109 F Street
South Boston, MA 02127

Emily Martin
742 7th Avenue
Iowa City, IA 52240

Pamela Moore
Codols 21, 3⁰, 1a,
08002 Barcelona
Spain

Louise Neaderland
Bone Hollow Arts
759 President Street, #2H
Brooklyn, NY 11215

Pamela Paulsrud
923 Amherst
Wilmette, IL 60091

Maria Pisano
6 Titus Lane
Plainsboro, NJ 08536

Lois Polansky
67 Short Way
Roslyn Heights, NY 11577-1963

Raven Regan
4825 Victory Street
Burnaby, BC, Canada
V5J 1S5

Mary Ann Sampson
P.O. Box 370
Ragland, AL 35131

David Schlater
P.O. Box 3701
Moscow, ID 83843

Susan Share
524 E. 15th Terrace, #PH,
Anchorage, AK 99501-5344

Laurie Snyder
5811 Merville Avenue
Baltimore, MD 21215

Indigo Som
P.O. Box 5053
Berkeley, CA 94705

Joan Soppe
650 28th Court S.E.
Cedar Rapids, IA 52403

Peter Sramek
79 Belsize Drive
Toronto, Ontario, Canada
M4S 1L3

Bonnie Stahlecker
6819 Sunrise Drive
Plainfield, IN 46168

Raymond H. Starr Jr.
11412 Marbrook Road
Owings Mills, MD 21117-2342

Phil Sultz
RR 1, Box 331
Dennysville, ME 04628-9801

Jill Timm
10610 Morado Circle #1021
Austin, TX 78759-5554

Kez van Oudheusden
30 Brooke Street
Clayfield, Queensland, Australia
4011

Deborah Waimon
1 Cherry Hill Lane
New Milford, CT 06776

KiP Walker
708 Canyon Road, #4
Santa Fe, NM 87501

index

About the Author

Author Kristina Feliciano is a former managing editor of
American Artist magazine and a freelance editor for The
New York Post. She has written on art, photography, and design
for numerous trade and news publications, is the editor of the
website drummergirl.com, and is a writer and editor for the
New York City-based Happy Mazza Media Company.